to Julia, Joli and Alan

Foreword

Once you have studied and begun to apply what Professor Ashlock so effectively teachers in this book, I am convinced you will agree it is among the most practical books you have ever encountered. It is practical for the immediate classroom as well as for long-term use.

One reason this book is immediately practical for classroom teachers is that it deals with real problems in a realistic manner. The types of errors in computation illustrated in this book are those of real children, and the suggested corrective procedures are those that have succeeded with real children. Moreover, both the procedures for diagnosis and those for correction require neither esoteric procedures nor specialized settings. The procedures are being used now successfully in the classroom.

Another reason this book is immediately practical is its clever organization. Chapter I sets the stage for the reader with a comprehensive, yet concise and thoroughly understandable, review of the research on children's computational errors. A discussion of how children learn these errors and a set of guidelines for diagnosing and treating difficulties in elementary school mathematics is also provided. Beginning in Chapter 2, and throughout the remainder of the book, the reader is cleverly led into participating directly in diagnosing and prescribing each of the error patterns illustrated. At each step, readers can "test" their diagnoses and prescriptions by comparing them with those Professor Ashlock and his students have found successful. The appendices in this new edition have additional suggestions for improving our diagnostic-prescriptive teaching of mathematics. It has been my experience using this book with both pre- and inservice teachers that this direct involvement not only helps them become proficient in diagnosing the specific errors illustrated, but also in becoming more adept at using the diagnostic-prescriptive process in all areas of the elementary school mathematics curriculum.

These immediately practical characteristics by themselves make this book well worth the reader's study. However, although not directly stated as a goal, I believe this book also contributes effectively to the clarification of two major issues which are of more long-term significance than just the identification and correlation of specific errors in computation.

All of us are aware of the considerable changes that have occurred in elementary school mathematics programs during the past two to three decades. Some have called these changes a "revolution." Two major interrelated issues have emerged during this revolution. One issue relates to the goals of elementary school mathematics education; the other relates to methods of instruction.

Among the most notable changes in the goals has been a greatly increased emphasis on the acquistion of mathematical concepts and principles, i.e., the learning of the structure of mathematics   qua   mathematics. In our eagerness to achieve this goal some programs have significantly deemphasized the achievement of computational proficiency. Some even took these two goals to be mutually exclusive.

In the late sixties and early seventies, as reports began to come in of children's falling scores on tests of computational skills, we began to hear from many quarters the demand to "return to the basics." This generally meant more work on adding, subtracting, multiplying, and dividing with skill. For many this "return to the basics" also meant a return to instructional methods thought appropriate to basic skills, i.e., lots and lots of practice or drill.

For many these issues have become dichotomies: mathematical concepts vs. computational skill; teaching for understanding vs. drill. Professor Ashlock's book, I believe, clearly demonstrates that to separate mathematical concepts from computational skill as goals and to separate the teaching for meaning from the administration of drill as methods are both false dichotomies.

The computational procedures in which we want children to be skillful only work because they are based on mathematical concepts and principles. The children's errors illustrated in this book clearly show this in reverse. All of the errors are based on *faulty* or incompletely learned mathematical concepts. Hence, all the corrective procedures involve developing or redeveloping these mathematical concepts.

Furthermore, Professor Ashlock clearly demonstrates that the patterns of error children display are not due to carelessness alone nor to insufficient drill. These error patterns are conceptual and are learned. Concepts, correct or incorrect, are not learned by drill. Once correct concepts are acquired, drill does help fix or consolidate that learning. Therefore, drill is a desirable and important component of instructional method — but only *after* the concepts have been acquired. It follows, then, that "just more practice," is not going to help the child identify his/her errors, nor is it going to help the child learn to correct them. Indeed, just more drill without meaningful, corrective instruction first is very likely to consolidate any error pattern a child has learned, thereby making it more difficult to correct.

This book helps put these two false dichotomies to rest. We can then get on with the task of helping children acquire skill in computation by teaching the mathematical concepts upon which computational procedures are based. Professor Ashlock's book with its immediately practical features helps us in this task as few others do.

John W. Wilson
University of Maryland

Preface

This book is designed for those who want to help children learn to compute. The reader learns to identify error patterns in computation, and he also learns about possible causes of such errors. Specific help for children who need to learn to compute successfully is described.

The patterns of error in computation which are included in this book are not figments of my imagination; they are patterns which have been observed in use by real boys and girls, children in regular classrooms. The problems in diagnosis posed for the reader are typical of difficulties encountered among those children everywhere who have difficulty with arithmetic.

The format of chapters 2, 3, and 4 has the advantages of simulation. Furthermore, the reader has opportunities to respond overtly; feedback is provided relating to those responses. Skill is gained by actually looking for patterns, making decisions, and planning instruction.

The introductory chapter contains specific suggestions as well as helpful guidelines for anyone who would help children learn to compute. Most readers will use chapters 2, 3, and 4 by topic, beginning in chapter 2 and turning to later parts of the book as instructed in the programs. It is important that the reader "play the game" and actually take time to respond.

I wish to acknowledge the encouragement of the many classroom teachers who have shown great interest in the material in this book, and the help of teachers who have identified many of the error patterns presented.

Robert B. Ashlock

Contents

1 Diagnosing and Correcting Errors in Computation 1

Research on Errors in Computation, 2

Why Children Learn Patterns of Error, 4

Guidelines for Diagnosis, 6

Guidelines for Remediation, 7

Mystery of Basic Facts, 10

Alternative Algorithms, 11

Preventing Patterns of Error, 15

2 Identifying Error Patterns in Computation 19

3 Analyzing Error Patterns in Computation 53

4 Helping Children Correct Error Pattens in Computation 83

Selected References 122

References Focusing on Diagnostic Tasks, 122 122

References Focusing on Remedial Tasks, 125 125

Appendix A Additional Children's Papers 129

Appendix B The Nature of Wrong Answers 135

Appendix C Helping Children Understand Our Numeration System 140

Appendix D Sample Learning Hierarchy for Addition of Unlike Fractions 142

Appendix E Selected Materials for Remedial Instruction 143

Diagnosing and Correcting Errors in Computation

Arithmetic is where the answer is right and
everything is nice and you can look out of the window
and see blue sky—or the answer is wrong and you have
to start all over and try again and see how it comes
out this time.[1]

Carl Sandburg

The child into whose mind Sandburg leads us seems to view arithmetic as an *either–or* sort of thing. Either he gets the right answers and he enjoys arithmetic and life is rosy, or he does not get the right answers and arithmetic and life are frustrating. You may think this child has a very limited view of arithmetic, and you may wonder why he is so answer-oriented. Yet, you *do* need to face the question of why some children are not able to get correct answers.

The diagnosis of errors in arithmetic is an essential part of evaluation in the mathematics program, and any such diagnosis must be accompanied by remedial or corrective instruction. It is hoped that reading this book will help you develop some of the skills needed for effective diagnosis and remediation of errors in computation.

If the written work of a child is to provide useful information for diagnosis, that work must not only be scored, it must be analyzed as well. The teacher needs to observe what the child does and does not do; he needs to note the computation which has correct answers and the computation which does not have correct answers; and he should look for those procedures used by the child which might be

---

[1] From "Arithmetic" in COMPLETE POEMS, copyright, 1950, by Carl Sandburg. Reprinted by permission of Harcourt Brace Jovanovich, Inc.

called mature and those which are less mature.[2] Usual scoring techniques do not distinguish among *procedures* used to get correct answers; frequently they do not even distinguish between situations in which the child uses an incorrect procedure and situations in which the child does not know how to proceed at all. Clearly an analysis of written work is needed. Many times it is possible for children to mark which examples are correct or incorrect. It is better to spend your time as a professional in analyzing the written work of children and planning corrective instruction than in using what time you have for scoring.

Research on Errors in Computation

Errors in computation are not necessarily just the result of carelessness or not knowing how to proceed. In a study of written computation, Roberts identified four error categories or "failure strategies." [3]

1. *Wrong operation:* The pupil attempts to respond by performing an operation other than the one that is required to solve the problem.
2. *Obvious computational error:* The pupil applies the correct operation, but his response is based on error in recalling basic number facts.
3. *Defective algorithm:* [4] The pupil attempts to apply the correct operation but makes errors other than number fact errors in carrying through the necessary steps.
4. *Random response:* The response shows no discernible relationship to the given problem.

Roberts noted that careless numerical errors and lack of familiarity with the addition and multiplication tables occurred with near-equal frequency at all ability levels. However, using the wrong operation and making random responses were observed more frequently with students of low ability and progressively less frequently with students of higher and higher ability. *The largest number of errors was due to erroneous or incorrect algorithm techniques* in all groups except the lowest quartile, which had more random responses. Note that incorrect algorithms were used by even the most able achievers (39 percent of the errors made by the upper quartile of pupils studied). Other researchers have made similar observations. Schacht concluded that "differences in performance appear to be of degree and not of kind, with the less able making errors more frequently than the more able."[5] Clearly, the practice papers of *all* pupils must be considered carefully.

---

[2] See John W. Wilson, "Diagnosis and Treatment in Mathematics: Its Progress, Problems, and Potential Role in Educating Emotionally Disturbed Children and Youth," in *The Teaching-Learning Process in Educating Emotionally Disturbed Children,* ed. Peter Knoblock and John L. Johnson (Syracuse, N.Y.: Syracuse University, Division of Special Education and Rehabilitation, 1967), p. 96.

[3] Gerhard H. Roberts, "The Failure Strategies of Third Grade Arithmetic Pupils," *The Arithmetic Teacher,* 15 (May 1968):442–46 .

[4] An algorithm is a step-by-step written procedure for determining the result of an arithmetic operation (*i.e.,* a sum, a difference, a product, or a quotient). A variety of algorithms or computational procedures can be used to determine any one missing number; and indeed, at different times and in different parts of the world, many differing but useful algorithms are taught. However, the algorithm used by a child is said to be "incorrect" or "defective" if the procedure does not always produce the correct result.

[5] Elmer J. Schacht, "A Study of the Mathematical Errors of Low Achievers in Elementary School Mathematics," *Dissertation Abstracts* 28A (September 1967): 920-21.

Brueckner did extensive work identifying types of errors in computation as early as the 1920s. These studies were reported in journals, in his classic 1930 text,[6] and in yearbook articles.[7] He stressed the importance of analyzing written work but also emphasized the need to supplement such activity with interviews. His study of difficulties children have when computing with decimals is characteristic of his research. This report, published in 1928, includes the tabulation of 8785 errors into 114 different kinds.[8] However, many of his categories are ambiguous, and some we would question today, for he listed the annexation of unnecessary zeros as an error and considered the vocalization of procedures a faulty habit. His class summaries of error types, though useless as far as providing help for an individual child, *do* alert us to the kinds of errors we need to forestall.

Others have described categories of errors in computation. Guiler noted that in the addition and subtraction of decimals, seven times as many children had trouble with the computation per se than had trouble with the decimal phases of the process. Further, in division of decimals, more than 40 percent of the children placed the decimal point three or more places too far to the right.[9] Such studies remind us of the value of a thorough understanding of numeration and the ability to estimate. Arthur, in a study of difficulties with arithmetic found among high school students, included types of errors such as adding denominators when adding fractions and failing to invert the divisor when dividing fractions.[10] He concluded that the reteaching of arithmetic skills should be based upon short diagnostic tests and given attention in all high school math classes. Cox concluded from her research that not only did children make systematic errors but, without instructional intervention, they continued with the error patterns for long periods of time.[11]

The most thorough study of errors in computation done in recent years is Lankford's study of seventh graders. [12] He conducted "diagnostic interviews" of 176 pupils in six schools located in different parts of the United States. The detailed report of the research includes many examples of the use of erroneous algorithms and the frequency of their occurrence among pupils in the study. Lankford's general observations concerning how wrong answers were derived for whole numbers and fractions are included in this text as Appendix B. In his conclusions he notes that "Unorthodox

---

[6]Leo J. Brueckner, *Diagnostic and Remedial Teaching in Arithmetic* (Philadelphia: John C. Winston Co., 1930).

[7]For example, his "Diagnosis in Arithmetic," in *Educational Diagnosis,* 34th Yearbook, National Society for the Study of Education (Bloomington, Ill.: Public School Publishing Co., 1935), pp. 269-302.

[8]Leo J. Brueckner, "Analysis of Difficulties in Decimals," *Elementary School Journal* 29 (September 1938): 32–41.

[9]Walter S. Guiler, "Difficulties in Decimals Encountered in Ninth-Grade Pupils," *Elementary School Journal* 46 (March 1946): 384–93.

[10]Lee E. Arthur, "Diagnosis of Disabilities in Arithmetic Essentials," *The Mathematics Teacher* 43 (May 1950): 197–202.

[11]L. S. Cox, "Diagnosing and Remediating Systematic Errors in Addition and Subtraction Computations," *The Arithmetic Teacher* 22 (February 1975): 151–57.

[12]Francis G. Lankford, Jr., *Some Computational Strategies of Seventh Grade Pupils,* U. S. Department of Health, Education, and Welfare, Office of Education, National Center for Educational Research and Development (Regional Research Program) and The Center for Advanced Study, The University of Virginia, October 1972. (Project number 2-C-013, Grant number OEG-3-72-0035)

strategies were frequently observed—some yielding correct answers and some incorrect ones."[13]

Why Children Learn Patterns of Error

How do children learn concepts and procedures? Children's mathematical ideas and computational procedures may be correct or erroneous, but the *process* of abstracting those ideas and procedures is basically the same. From a set of experiences with a concept or a process, a child pulls out or abstracts those things which the experiences have in common. The intersection of the experiences defines the idea or process for the child.

If a child's only experiences with the idea *five* are with manila cards having black dots in the familiar domino pattern (see Figure 1a), he may abstract from these experiences a notion of five which includes many or all of the characteristics his experiences have had in common. The ideas of black on manila paper, round dots, or a specific configuration may become part of the child's idea of five. One of the author's students, when presenting to children the configuration associated with Stern pattern boards (see Figure 1b) was told, "That's not five. Five doesn't look like that."

More children will name as a triangle the shape in Figure 1c than the shape in Figure 1d; yet both are triangles. Again, configuration (or even the orientation of the figure) may be a common characteristic of the child's limited range of experiences with triangles.

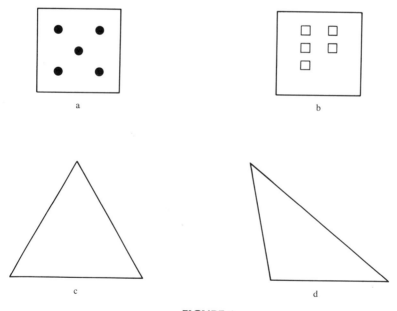

a

b

c

d

FIGURE 1

Dr. Geoffrey Matthews, organizer of the Nuffield Mathematics Teaching Project in England, tells of a child who computed correctly one year but missed about half

---

[13]*Ibid.*, p. 40.

of the problems the next year. As the child learned to compute, he adopted the rule, "Begin on the side by the piano." The next school year the child was in a room with the piano on the other side, and he was understandably confused about where to start computing.

When multiplication of fractions (or rational numbers) is introduced, children frequently have difficulty believing their correct answers make sense because throughout their previous experiences with factors and products the product was always at least as large as the smaller factor. (Actually, the product is noticeably larger than either factor in most cases.) In the mind of the child, the concept of product had come to include the idea of larger number because this was common throughout most of his experiences with products. This may be one reason many children have difficulty with the zero property for multiplication of whole numbers. The product zero is usually smaller than one of the factors.

Creature Cards also illustrate this view of concept formation (see Figure 2). The child confronted with a Creature Card is given a name or label such as Gruffle and told to decide what Gruffle is. He looks for common characteristics among a set of Gruffles. Then, experiences with non-Gruffles help him eliminate from consideration those characteristics which happen to be common in the set of Gruffles but are

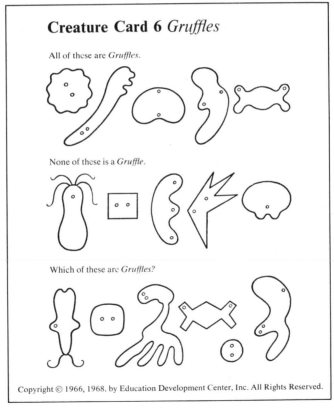

SOURCE: Reproduced from the Elementary Science Study unit, *Attribute Games and Problems*, by permission of Education Development Center, Inc.

FIGURE 2

not essential to "Gruffleness" (i.e., the definition of a Gruffle would not include such attributes). Finally, the cards provide an opportunity for the child to test out his newly derived definition.

Children often learn erroneous concepts and processes similarly. They look for commonalities among their initial contacts with the idea of procedure. They pull out or abstract certain common characteristics, and their concept or algorithm is formed. The common attributes may be very specific, such as, crossing out a digit, placing a digit in front of another, or finding the difference between two one-digit numbers (regardless of order). From time to time such inadequate procedures even produce correct answers. When this happens, use of the erroneous procedure is reinforced for the child who is anxious to succeed. The child who decides that rounding whole numbers to the nearest ten means erasing the units digit and writing a zero is correct about half of the time! After observing similar "discoveries" by children, the psychologist Friedlander noted that as teachers "seek to capitalize on the students' reasoning, errors of fact, of perception, or of association can lead to hopelessly chaotic chains of mistaken inferences and deductions."[14]

There are many reasons why children are prone to overgeneralize and learn patterns of error. It most certainly is not the intentional result of instructions. Yet all too often, especially when taught in groups, children do not have prerequisite understandings and skills they need when introduced to new ideas and procedures. When this happens, they want to please the teacher (or at least survive in the situation); so they tend to "grab at straws." Furthermore, teachers who introduce paper-and-pencil procedures while a child still needs to work problems out with concrete aids are encouraging the child to try to memorize a complex sequence of mechanical acts. This, again, prompts the child to adopt simplistic procedures he can remember. Because incorrect algorithms do not usually result in correct answers, it would appear that a child receives limited positive reinforcement for continued use of erroneous procedures. However, children sometimes hold tenaciously to incorrect procedures even during remedial instruction. Each incorrect algorithm is an interesting study in itself, and in succeeding sections of this book you will have opportunities to identify several erroneous computational procedures and consider possible reasons for adoption of such procedures by children.

Guidelines for Diagnosis

> A plan in the heart of a man is like deep water,
> But a man of understanding draws it out.[15]

As you work diagnostically with students, seeking to determine the extent and nature of errors and possible causes of those errors, you must be careful to apply what has already been learned about making diagnoses. The following guidelines provide a brief summary of principles to keep in mind as you work with children having difficulty with computation.

---

[14]Bernard Z. Friedlander, "A Psychologist's Second Thoughts on Concepts, Curiosity, and Discovery in Teaching and Learning," *Harvard Educational Review* 35 (Winter 1965): 29.
[15]Proverbs 20:5, *New American Standard Bible*, The Lockman Foundation, 1971.

1. *Be Accepting.* Diagnosis is a highly personal process. Before a child will cooperate with you as his teacher in a manner which may lead to lessening or elimination of his problems with computation, he must perceive that you are interested in and respect him as a person, that you are genuinely interested in helping him, and that you are quite willing to accept a response even when the response is not correct. In short, if sufficient data are to be collected for an adequate diagnosis, the child must understand that you are willing to accept his failures. You must exhibit something of the attitude of a good physician toward his patient, and, as Tournier, a Swiss physician, has noted, "What antagonizes a patient is not the truth, but the tone of scorn, pity, criticism, or reproof which so often colors the statement of the truth by those around him."[16]

2. *Collect Data—Do Not Instruct.* In making a diagnosis, you must differentiate between the role of collecting data (testing) and the role of teaching. Diagnosing involves gathering as much useful data as possible and making judgments on the basis of the data collected; in general, the more data, the more adequate the judgments which follow. The child is apt to provide many samples of incorrect and immature procedures if he sees that you are merely collecting information which will be used to help him overcome his difficulties. However, if you point out errors, label responses as "wrong," and offer instruction, the child is far less likely to expose his own inadequate performance. When a teacher who usually offers help as soon as he sees incorrect or immature performance begins to distinguish between collecting data and instruction, he is often delighted with the way children begin to open up and lay bare their thinking.

3. *Be Thorough.* A given diagnosis is rarely thorough enough to provide direction for continuing remediation. From time to time it is necessary to have short periods of diagnosis even during remedial instruction. In fact, if you are alert during the instruction which follows a diagnosis, you may pick up cues which suggest additional diagnostic activities apt to provide helpful data about the child and his problem.

4. *Look for Patterns.* Data should be evaluated in terms of patterns, not isolated events. A decision about remedial instruction can hardly be based upon collected bits of unrelated information. As you look for patterns you engage in a kind of problem-solving activity, for you yourself look for elements common to several examples of a child's work. Look for repeated applications of erroneous definitions and try to find consistent use of incorrect or immature procedures. The importance of looking for patterns can hardly be overstressed, for many erroneous procedures are practiced by children while their teachers assume the children are merely careless or "don't know their facts."

Guidelines for Remediation

When you begin to find patterns of errors in a child's computation, your thoughts should turn to the task of providing remedial instruction. You want to correct erroneous procedures and lead the child into more mature ways of dealing with

---

[16]Paul Tournier, *The Healing of Persons* (New York: Harper and Row, 1965), p. 243.

number situations. Above all, you want the child to experience success instead of failure. The following guidelines which clinicians have found quite applicable to their work with arithmetic underachievers incorporate many principles which you should keep in mind as you provide corrective instruction.

1. *Encourage self-appraisal by the child.* From the beginning, involve him in the evaluation process. Let the child help set the goals of instruction.

2. *Make sure the child has the goals of instruction clearly in mind.* Take care to ensure that he knows the behavior that is needed on his part, for the child needs to know where he is headed. He needs to know where he is headed eventually ("I'll be able to subtract and get the right answers"), but he also needs to know where he is headed immediately ("I'll soon be able to rename a number many different ways").

3. *Let the child state his understanding of a concept in his own language.* Do not always require the terminology of textbooks. It may be appropriate to say, for example, "Mathematicians have a special name for that idea, but I rather like your name for it!"

4. *Protect and strengthen the child's self-image.* A child who has met repeated failure needs to believe that he is a valued person and that he is capable of eventually acquiring the needed skill.

5. *Structure instruction in small steps.* A large task may seem overwhelming to a child. However, when instruction is based upon a carefully determined sequence of smaller steps that lead to the larger task, the child can focus on more immediately attainable goals. He can also be helped to see that the immediate goals lead along a path going in the desired direction.

6. *Select practice activities which provide immediate confirmation.* When looking for games and drill activities to strengthen skills, choose those activities which let the child know immediately if his answer is correct. Many games, manipulative devices, programmed materials, and teacher-made devices provide such reinforcement.

7. *Spread practice time over several short periods.* A given amount of time spent in drill activities is usually more fruitful if distributed over short periods. A short series of examples (perhaps five to eight) is usually adequate to observe any error pattern. Longer series tend to reinforce erroneous procedures. If a correct procedure *is* being used, then frequent practice with a limited number of examples is more fruitful than occasional practice with a large number of examples.

8. *Use a great variety of instructional procedures and activities.* Variety is necessary for adequate concept development. A child forms an idea or concept from many experiences embodying that idea; he perceives the concept as that which is common to all of the varied experiences.

9. *Provide the child with a means to observe his progress.* Charts and graphs kept by the child often serve this function.

10. *Choose instructional procedures that differ from the way the child was previously taught.* The old procedures are often associated with fear and failure by the child; something new is needed.

11. *Encourage a child to use aids as long as they are of value.* Peer group pressure often keeps a child from using an aid even when the teacher places such aids on a table. The use of aids needs to be encouraged actively. At times a child needs to be encouraged to try thinking a process through with just paper and pencil, but by and large children give up aids when they feel safe without them. After all, the use of aids is time-consuming.

12. *Let the child choose from materials available.* Whenever possible, the child should be permitted to select a game or activity from materials which are available and which lead toward the goals of instruction. Identify activities for which the child has needed prerequisite skills and which lead to the goals of instruction; then let the child have some choice in deciding what he will do.

13. *Emphasize underlying concepts and procedures.* For most children, it is necessary that they have a firm understanding of subordinate mathematical concepts before they can be expected to integrate these into more complex ideas.[17]

14. *Emphasize ideas which help the child organize what he learns.* New learnings need to be tied in with what a child already knows so that the new learnings will be meaningful. When so organized, new learnings can be more easily retrieved from a child's memory as the need arises. Stress ideas such as multiple names for a number, commutativity, identity elements, and inverse relations.

15. *Stress the ability to estimate.* A child who makes errors in computation will become more accurate as he is able to determine the reasonableness of his answers. Estimating is discussed further in a later section.

An additional word about the use of drill or practice activities may be helpful. We have known for some time that, in general, drill reinforces and makes more efficient that which a child *actually* practices.[18] In other words, if a child counts on his fingers to find a sum, drill will only tend to help him count on his fingers more efficiently. He may find sums more quickly, but he is apt to continue any immature procedure he is using. You stand forewarned against the use of extensive practice activities at a time when they merely reinforce processes which are developmental.

---

[17]See Leroy Callahan, "Remedial Work with Underachieving Children," *The Arithmetic Teacher* 9 (March 1962): 138-40. Also, the writings of Robert Gagné will help you acquire the ability to identify subordinate concepts and skills for a given mathematical task. For example, see "Learning and Proficiency in Mathematics," *The Mathematics Teacher* 56 (December 1963): 620-26; also in Robert B. Ashlock and Wayne L. Herman, Jr., *Current Research in Elementary School Mathematics* (New York: The Macmillan Co., 1970), pp. 55-63. Similar help is available in Henry H. Walbesser, *Constructing Behavioral Objectives* (College Park, Maryland: Bureau of Educational Research and Field Services, College of Education, University of Maryland, 1968).

[18]See William A. Brownell and Charlotte B. Chazel, "The Effects of Premature Drill in Third Grade Arithmetic," *The Journal of Educational Research* 29 (September 1935): 17–28ff; also in Robert B. Ashlock and Wayne L. Herman, Jr., *Current Research in Elementary School Mathematics* (New York: The Macmillan Co., 1970), pp. 170–88.

Drill for mastery should come when the actual process being practiced is an efficient process. Admittedly, it is not always easy to determine what process is actually being practiced. By looking for patterns of error and by conducting data-gathering interviews in an atmosphere in which a child's failures are accepted, you can usually learn enough to decide if a child is ready for more extensive practice.

Mastery of Basic Facts

A problem encountered frequently when helping a child learn to compute is the child's inability to recall the basic facts of arithmetic without resorting to counting or repeated use of addition or another procedure. The *basic facts* of arithmetic are the simple, closed number sentences we use when we compute. These number sentences involve two one-digit addends if they are basic addition or subtraction facts, or two one-digit factors if they are basic multiplication or division facts. They are sometimes called the "primary facts." Examples of the basic facts of arithmetic include the following:

$$6 + 7 = 13 \qquad 12 - 8 = 4 \qquad 3 \times 5 = 15 \qquad 27 \div 9 = 3$$

Mastery of the basic facts of arithmetic is the ability to supply missing sums, addends, products, and factors for these basic facts promptly and without hesitation. The child who has mastered the basic fact "$6 + 8 = 14$" will, when presented with "$6 + 8 = ?$," simply recall "14" without counting or figuring it out. When a child is learning how to find the product of any two whole number factors (such as "36×457") by using one of the appropriate computation procedures, any lack of mastery of the basic multiplication facts results in the child using time-consuming and distracting ways of finding needed basic products. As a result, the child's attention is drawn from the larger task of thinking through the computational procedure for multiplication. He is often uncertain about where he is in the process and frequently he proceeds at random, having lost his way. If a child is to use arithmetic to solve quantitative problems, it is important that he master the basic facts of arithmetic.

To say that mastery is important should not imply that it is necessarily easy. Consider the child who is in need of remedial instruction. In all probability he has already met considerable failure in learning to compute and regards the whole matter with notable anxiety. Biggs has observed that "In arithmetic and mathematics, the inhibition produced by anxiety appears to swamp any motivating effect, particularly where the children concerned are already anxious; or to put it another way, anxiety appears to be more easily aroused in learning mathematics than it is in other subjects."[19]

If the child has not mastered the basic facts of arithmetic, he probably persists in using counting or elaborate procedures for finding the needed numbers. He may understand the operations on whole numbers in terms of joining disjoint sets, repeated additions, etc., yet he continues to require the security of counting or other

---

[19]John Biggs, "The Psychopathology of Arithmetic," in *New Approaches to Mathematics Teaching,* ed. F. W. Land (London: Macmillan & Co., 1963), p. 59.

time-consuming procedures. Such a child does not trust himself simply to recall the number. He has practiced computing, but he has only reinforced his use of less than adequate procedures. The danger of extensive practice when the processes being practiced are developmental rather than the desired efficient practices has been noted. What is needed is practice recalling the number; practice "figuring it out" could do more harm than good.

How then can you provide instructional activities that create an environment in which a child feels secure enough to try recalling missing numbers? Games provide the safest environment for simple recall, for when playing games, someone has to lose. Where the teacher always seems to want "the right answer," in a game it is acceptable to lose at least part of the time. The competition in a game encourages a child to use the least time-consuming procedure and to try simply recalling needed numbers. Further, games often make possible greater attending behavior by a child because of the materials involved in the game itself. For example, a child who rejects a paper-and-pencil problem such as "$6 + 5 = ?$" because it reminds him of failure and unpleasantness may attend with interest when the same problem is presented with numerals painted on brightly colored cubes which he moves about.

Obviously, what is intended is *not* the kind of arithmetic game modeled after an old-fashioned spelling bee designed to eliminate the less able children. Nor is it a game designed to put a child under pressure in front of a large group of peers. The best games will be games involving only a few children, preferably children of rather comparable ability. In such games a child can feel secure enough to try simple recall. Games which provide immediate or early verification should be chosen. The child should learn as soon as possible if he did indeed recall correctly. Many commercial games are available, but games can be made up using materials already in the classroom or simple homemade materials. Children are quite capable of making up games and altering the rules of games to suit their own fancy when they are encouraged to do so. For example, a homemade game using mathematical balances would provide immediate verification for each child's response (see Figure 3).

When working privately with a child who is very insecure and insists on continuing to use elaborate procedures for "figuring out" his basic facts, it may help to change the ground rules and dismiss "getting the correct answer." Try letting the child say the first number that he thinks of after hearing or seeing the problem. Chances are he'll be correct many times and you can show considerable surprise that he "pulled the correct answer right out of his head." In such a setting, some children have been helped to practice recalling where they did not feel able to recall before.

Alternative Algorithms

Another remedial approach involves the use of a variety of computational procedures. If you are really willing to accept the idea that there are many legitimate ways to subtract, divide, and so on, you may choose to introduce a child having difficulty to an algorithm which is fresh and new to him. By so doing, you may circumvent the mind set of failure which beleaguers the child. But if you are convinced that there is really only one "right" way to subtract or divide, you will have no

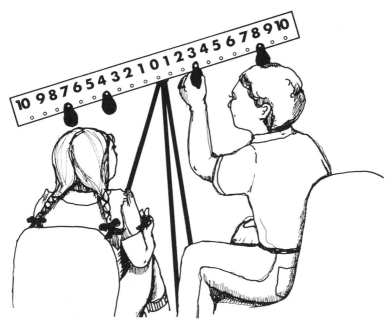

FIGURE 3

heart for introducing alternative computational procedures. When the immediate need of the child is for successful experience in mathematics, the use of alternative algorithms holds promise, but you should first face yourself squarely and make sure you can heartily endorse such computational procedures as having value in themselves apart from any "right" way of computing. If you believe you are leading the child to an inferior technique, he will sense your feeling.

An important question arises when you decide to show a child an alternate computational procedure, for many of the algorithms which have been employed through the centuries have been used much as you would use a machine—without knowledge of why the procedure produces the correct result. Indeed, many of the algorithms of historical interest are quite difficult to explain mathematically. As you will see, some of the alternatives available can be shown to make sense, but, in your work with an unsuccessful child, many of the alternatives will be learned only as a machine to use when a result is needed. The difficult question remains, Do you only present algorithms which will make sense, or do you sometimes teach a child how to use a machine?

I am convinced of the need to teach for "meaningful computation." In view of the evidence reported in our research literature, any other conviction would hardly be warranted. Meaningful instruction is needed not just for the able child, but also for the slow-learning child. At the same time, remember that when planning remedial instruction you are sometimes dealing with a child who has known much failure and who will not really attend to instruction similar to his past unhappy experiences. In order to secure the interest and attention of such a child, very different instructional procedures are needed. Further, it may be that the *most* important need for the child is to get a *correct* answer, to experience success. In view of these considerations, there are times when a computational procedure *which is fresh and new to the child* can be taught as a machine to use whenever a result is needed. If the child learns and remembers the procedure, the needed success experience has been provided. If he does not, then the procedure can be set aside much as you would set aside anything else you try and do not like. Interestingly, alternative algorithms have always been explored unhesitatingly as enrichment or recreational activity.

What are some of the algorithms which can be used as alternatives when working remedially with a child? A few examples are described below, and others will be found in the literature of mathematics education and recreation.

Addition of Whole Numbers: The Tens Method[20]

$$\begin{array}{r} 468 \\ 793 \\ 809 \\ 986 \\ \hline 3058 \end{array}$$

The columns can be added downward or upward. Beginning at the top right in the example shown, 8 plus 5 equals 13, which can be renamed as 1 ten and 3 ones. A line is drawn through the 5 to show that it was the last digit used in obtaining ten. The ten does not need to be held in mind because the line represents it for us. Now, with the 3 which was left over, add until another ten is obtained. In this case 3 plus 9 equals 12, which can be renamed as 1 ten plus 2. Another line is drawn (through the 9) to indicate another ten. The sum of the 2 left over and 6 is 8, which is recorded as the unit's digit at the bottom of the column.

The two lines which are drawn in the units column represent 2 tens, and addition begins in the tens column by adding these 2 tens to the 6 tens and continuing until there is a sum greater than 10 tens; 2 tens plus 6 tens plus 9 tens equals 17 tens. A line is drawn through the 9 to represent 10 tens, and 7 tens remain. As we proceed, 7 plus 0 plus 8 equals 15; a line is drawn through the 8, and the 5 is recorded as the tens digit at the bottom.

In the tens column, each line represents 10 tens or 1 hundred. It is noted that there are two such lines, so 2 hundreds are added to the 4 hundreds in the next column; and addition proceeds similarly.

Addition of Whole Numbers: The Scratch Method

A. ↓	B. ↓	C.	D. ↓	E.
378	378	378	378	378
+294	+294	+294	+294	+294
5	5 6	5 6	5 6 2	5 6 2
	1	7	7 1 1	7 7
		6	6	6 7
				672

Addition proceeds from left to right. Numerals are "scratched out" in order to write the total number of hundreds, tens, and units as the computation proceeds.

[20]Elbert Fulkerson, "Adding by Tens," *The Arithmetic Teacher* 10 (March 1963): 139–40.

Subtraction of Whole Numbers: Hutchings's Low-stress Method[21]

A.
$$\begin{array}{r} 4352 \\ -\ 1826 \\ \hline \end{array}$$

B.
$$\begin{array}{r} 4352 \\ 42 \\ -1826 \\ \hline \end{array}$$

C.
$$\begin{array}{r} 4352 \\ 3\,3\ 4\,{}^{1}2 \\ -1826 \\ \hline \end{array}$$

D.
$$\begin{array}{r} 4352 \\ 3\,3\ 4\,{}^{1}2 \\ -1826 \\ \hline 2526 \end{array}$$

This algorithm has been shown to be an especially effective procedure for remedial use. Note that the minuend (sum) is renamed with the help of half-space digits, and the renamed minuend is written between the given minuend and the subtrahend (know addend). All renaming is completed before subtraction facts are recalled.

Subtraction of Whole Numbers: The Equal-Additions Method

A.
$$\begin{array}{r} 4 5\overset{\downarrow}{3} \\ -\ 1_{8}\cancel{7}\,8 \\ \hline 5 \end{array}$$

B.
$$\begin{array}{r} 4\,{}'5\,{}'3 \\ {}_{2}\cancel{1}_{8}\cancel{7}\,8 \\ \hline 275 \end{array}$$

The principle of compensation is applied; equal quantities are added to both the minuend and the subtrahend in order to use basic subtraction facts. Ten is added to the sum, *i.e.*, to the three in the ones place. To compensate for this addition, ten is also added to the known addend; the seven in the tens place is replaced with an eight. Similarly, 1 hundred is added to the sum, *i.e.*, the five in the tens place becomes a fifteen. To compensate, 1 hundred is added to the known addend; the one in the hundreds place is replaced with a two.

Multiplication of Whole Numbers: The Lattice Method

Problem:
$$\begin{array}{r} 627 \\ \times\ 354 \\ \hline \end{array}$$

Product: 221,958

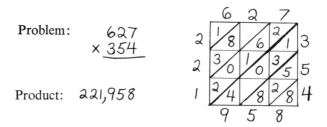

[21]Lloyd B. Hutchings, "Low-stress Subtraction," *The Arithmetic Teacher* 22 (March 1975): 226–32.

The two factors are written above and to the right of a grid. The products of basic multiplication facts are recorded within the grid, and addition proceeds from upper right to lower left within the diagonal lines. The final product is read at the left and at the bottom of the grid.

Division of Whole Numbers: The Doubling Method[22]

Problem: $290 \div 8 = ?$

Quotient: $36\,r2$

$$8 \times 1 = 8$$
$$8 \times 2 = 16$$
$$8 \times 4 = 32$$
$$8 \times 8 = 64$$
$$8 \times 16 = 128$$
$$8 \times 32 = 256$$

$$\begin{array}{r} 290 \\ -256 \leftarrow 32 \\ \hline 34 \\ 32 \leftarrow 4 \\ \hline 2 \quad 36 \end{array}$$

The divisor is doubled until the next double would be larger than the dividend, thereby determining the largest partial quotient. Smaller partial quotients are determined for the part of the dividend remaining. Finally, the partial quotients are added to determine the quotient.

The most useful alternative algorithms for children having difficulty with computation are probably algorithms which separate fact recall and regrouping in order to reduce the amount of remembering required. Examples of such low-stress algorithms are being developed for each of the whole number operations by Dr. Lloyd Barton Hutchings. Research with Hutchings' algorithms suggests that they should be especially helpful for remedial work with low achievers.

Preventing Patterns of Error

As you become increasingly aware of patterns of errors in the written work of children and as you reflect upon why children begin using such procedures, you will also begin to ponder the question, "What can I do to make sure my pupils learn *correct* computational procedures and not these erroneous procedures?" You will want to teach in a way which makes the adoption of erroneous procedures a very unlikely event!

What is needed is thorough, developmental instruction in which it is possible for each child to move through a carefully planned sequence of different types of learning activities. The amount of time needed for each type of activity will vary from child to child, and, for any one individual, the pace will likely vary from day to day. If you are to lessen the likelihood that children learn patterns of error, you will have to resist the temptation to cover the text or the curriculum guide by completing two pages a day or some similar plan. Careful attention will have to be given to ideas and skills needed by each child in order to learn the concept or algorithm under study. This is why the first step in a learning sequence should be diagnostic in nature.

---

[22]C. Alan Riedesel, *Guiding Discovery in Elementary School Mathematics* (New York: Appleton-Century-Crofts, 1967), pp. 199–200.

TABLE I.
Flow Chart of the Learning Sequence

Step	Purpose	Activities	Materials
1 Preparation	To provide readiness: both subject-matter — including prerequisite skills, vocabulary, and concepts—and interest.	A checkup—formal or informal—on prerequisite skills and vocabulary.	Tests, if necessary, teacher-made or commercial. Models, real objects, and other learning aids as necessary.
2 Exploration and discovery	To lead the pupil to develop the concept (or operation) as a solution to a problem situation.	Presenting a stimulating problem situation requiring improvisation of the process, concept, or operation as a means of solution.	Learning aids as needed to provide the setting. Materials as required for manipulation in exploratory activities.
3 Abstraction and organization	To develop an understanding of the nature of the operation (or concept)and its interrelationship with other operations.	Development of generalizations about the operation (or concept) and its interrelationships to others.	Textbooks and semisymbolic manipulative materials.
4 Fixing skills	To make manipulation of the operation automatic and to provide overlearning to assure retention.	Memorization of facts, organization and memorization of tables, and repetitive practice with the operation.	Textbooks, practice materials, and tests.
5 Application	To promote transfer of training by developing ability to recognize the typical situations calling for use of the operation (or concept).	Experience in application to a variety of situations, with emphasis on identifying the appropriate situations.	Life and simulated problem situations: models, visual aids, textbooks, and bulletin boards.

SOURCE: From *Teaching Elementary School Mathematics for Understanding* by John L. Marks, E. Richard Purdy, and Lucien B. Kinney. Copyright 1970 by McGraw-Hill. Used with permission of McGraw-Hill Book Co.

What other purposes do learning activities need to serve in a thorough program of instruction? A helpful sequence of five steps, as described by Marks, Purdy, and Kinney, appears in Table I. It is important to realize that activities may take many forms at each step in the sequence. For example, learning centers can be designed for each step in the learning sequence, and, similarly, manipulative aids can be used at each step.

When choosing manipulative materials, you need to keep in mind the need for varied exemplars. It has already been noted that children look for commonalities among their contacts with an idea or an algorithm, and, as they come to understand, they pull out or abstract the common characteristics among their experiences. Therefore, children need experiences in which all perceptual stimuli are varied except those which are essential to the mathematical idea or procedure. A cardboard place-value chart may be of great value, but it should not be the only exemplar you use for abstracting and organizing activities concerned with numeration. Other exemplars made with juice cans or wooden boxes should also be used. Similarly, at the symbolic level you need to take care to vary the examples. In a subtraction example like $42 - 17 = ?$, a child may conclude that the five units in the answer is simply the result of finding the difference between the two and the seven. Examples must be varied so that such characteristics are not common among examples under study.

It is frequently the case that a proper emphasis on estimation during instruction will eliminate much of the need for future remediation. One of the recommendations of the Lankford study cited previously was that teachers "give more attention to teaching pupils to check the reasonableness of answers."[23] And those who caution that the widespread availability of calculators will not eliminate the need for computational skills also stress the need for skill in estimation. "The calculator is designed to do only the keypuncher's bidding. Nor will the calculator tell whether or not an answer is reasonable. Estimation to judge the reasonableness of an answer will still require computational skill."[24]

Estimation can be emphasized by allowing children time to guess, test their guesses, and revise their guesses as needed. Children should be encouraged to develop their own ways of deciding when an answer is reasonable. It may be desirable to show them more standard procedures at a later time.

Estimating is itself a complex of skills, any one of which may require instruction and practice apart from the more general question "Is your answer reasonable?" Included among such skills are:

1. Adding a little bit more than one number to a little bit more than another; a little bit less than one number to a little bit less than another; and, similarly, adding, subtracting, etc., with a little bit more than or a little bit less than.

2. Rounding a whole number to the nearest ten, hundred, etc.

3. Multiplying by ten and powers of ten in one step.

4. Multiplying two numbers, each of which is a multiple of a power of ten (e.g., 20 x 300). This should be done as one step, without the use of an algorithm.

---

[23]Lankford, 1972, p. 42.

[24]Eugene P. Smith, "A Look at Mathematics Education Today," *The Arithmetic Teacher* 20 (October 1973): 505.

To practice estimating, children can be presented with a problem and several answers. They can then choose the answer which is most reasonable. If appropriate, their choice can be verified by computation. The practice of recording an estimated answer before computation should be encouraged. In general, children become more and more able to determine when an answer is reasonable as they gain the habit of asking if the answer makes sense, and as they progress from guessing to educated guessing to more specific estimating procedures. Children who have the habit of considering the reasonableness of their answers are not as prone to adopt incorrect computational procedures.

2

Identifying Error Patterns
in Computation

Remedial or corrective instruction should be based upon sufficient data to suggest patterns of incorrect and immature procedures. As a teacher of elementary school mathematics, you need to be alert to error patterns in computation. On the following pages you will find examples of the written work of boys and girls who are having difficulty with some phase of computation. With these simulated children's papers you have the opportunity to develop your own skill in identifying error patterns. However, these are more than simulated papers, for these papers contain the error patterns of real boys and girls, error patterns observed by my colleagues and me among children in regular elementary school classrooms. These are the children who may be in your own classroom.

As you examine each paper, look for a pattern of error; then check your findings by using the error pattern yourself with the examples provided. In other parts of this book you will learn if your observations are accurate and you will get feedback on your own suggestions for corrective instruction.

If this book is to help you with your teaching of elementary school mathematics, you will need to "play the game." Take time to try out the error pattern before turning on to another part of the book. Write out brief descriptions of instructional activities before moving ahead to see what suggestions are recorded later. Do not be content just to read about patterns of error; as a teacher you also learn by *doing*. Take time to respond in writing in the designated places. For further practice identifying error patterns, additional children's papers (and a key) can be found in Appendix A.

Error Pattern A-W-1

Examine Mike's work carefully. Can you find the error pattern he has followed?

Name _Mike_

A.
```
  74
+ 56
────
1210
```
B.
```
  35
+ 92
────
 127
```
C.
```
  67
+ 18
────
 715
```
D.
```
  56
+ 97
────
1413
```

Have you found the error pattern? Check yourself by using the error pattern to compute these examples.

E.
```
  43
+ 65
────
```
F.
```
  88
+ 39
────
```

Next, turn to pattern A-W-1 on page 54 to see if you were able to identify the error pattern. Why might Mike or any student use such an erroneous computational procedure?

Error Pattern A-W-2

What error pattern is Mary following in her written work?

Name *Mary*

A.
$$\begin{array}{r} 432 \\ +265 \\ \hline 697 \end{array}$$

B.
$$\begin{array}{r} 7\overset{\text{\tiny|}}{4} \\ +43 \\ \hline 18 \end{array}$$

C.
$$\begin{array}{r} 38\overset{4}{5} \\ +667 \\ \hline 9116 \end{array}$$

D.
$$\begin{array}{r} 5\overset{\circ}{6}\overset{\circ}{3} \\ +545 \\ \hline 118 \end{array}$$

Check to see if you found Mary's pattern by using her erroneous procedure to compute these examples.

E.
$$\begin{array}{r} 254 \\ +535 \end{array}$$

F.
$$\begin{array}{r} 618 \\ +782 \end{array}$$

Next, turn to page 55 to see if you were able to identify Mary's error pattern. Why might Mary or any child use such a procedure?

Error Pattern A-W-3

Carol gets some correct answers, but she seems to miss many of the easiest examples. See if you can find her error pattern.

Name *Carol*

A.
$$\begin{array}{r} 46 \\ +\ 3 \\ \hline 13 \end{array}$$
B.
$$\begin{array}{r} 18 \\ +30 \\ \hline 48 \end{array}$$
C.
$$\begin{array}{r} 8 \\ +16 \\ \hline 15 \end{array}$$
D.
$$\begin{array}{r} 42 \\ +56 \\ \hline 98 \end{array}$$
E.
$$\begin{array}{r} 74 \\ +\ 5 \\ \hline 16 \end{array}$$

Use Carol's procedure for these examples to make sure you have found her error pattern.

F.
$$\begin{array}{r} 26 \\ +\ 3 \\ \hline \end{array}$$
G.
$$\begin{array}{r} 60 \\ +24 \\ \hline \end{array}$$
H.
$$\begin{array}{r} 74 \\ +\ 5 \\ \hline \end{array}$$

When you have completed examples F, G, and H, turn to page 56. Why might Carol be using such a procedure?

Error Pattern A-W-4

Can you find Dorothy's pattern of errors?

Name *Dorothy*

A.
$$\begin{array}{r} \overset{1}{75} \\ +\ \ 8 \\ \hline 163 \end{array}$$

B.
$$\begin{array}{r} \overset{1}{67} \\ +\ 4 \\ \hline 111 \end{array}$$

C.
$$\begin{array}{r} \overset{1}{84} \\ +\ 9 \\ \hline 183 \end{array}$$

D.
$$\begin{array}{r} \overset{1}{59} \\ 6 \\ \hline 125 \end{array}$$

Did you find the pattern? Make sure by using the error pattern to compute these examples.

E.
$$\begin{array}{r} 46 \\ +\ \ 8 \\ \hline \end{array}$$

F.
$$\begin{array}{r} 98 \\ +\ 3 \\ \hline \end{array}$$

When you have completed examples E and F, turn to page 56 and see if you identified the pattern correctly. Why might Dorothy be using such a procedure?

Error Pattern S-W-1

Look carefully at Cheryl's written work. What error pattern has she followed?

Name _Cheryl_

A.
$$\begin{array}{r} 32 \\ -16 \\ \hline 16 \end{array}$$

B.
$$\begin{array}{r} 245 \\ -137 \\ \hline 112 \end{array}$$

C.
$$\begin{array}{r} 524 \\ -298 \\ \hline 374 \end{array}$$

D.
$$\begin{array}{r} 135 \\ -67 \\ \hline 132 \end{array}$$

If you have found the error pattern, check yourself by using the error pattern to compute these examples.

E.
$$\begin{array}{r} 458 \\ -372 \\ \hline \end{array}$$

F.
$$\begin{array}{r} 241 \\ -96 \\ \hline \end{array}$$

Now turn to pattern S-W-1 on page 57 to see if you were able to identify the error pattern. Why might a child use such a computational procedure?

Error Pattern S-W-2

Look over George's paper carefully. Can you find the error pattern he is using?

Name _George_

A.

$$\begin{array}{r} \overset{8}{1}\overset{\,1}{9}7 \\ -\ 43 \\ \hline 1414 \end{array}$$

B.

$$\begin{array}{r} \overset{6}{1}\overset{\,1}{7}6 \\ -\ 23 \\ \hline 1413 \end{array}$$

$$\begin{array}{r} \overset{7}{3}\overset{\,1}{8}4 \\ -\ 59 \\ \hline 325 \end{array}$$

Did you find the error pattern? Check yourself by using George's error pattern to compute examples D and E.

D.

$$\begin{array}{r} 273 \\ -\ 38 \\ \hline \end{array}$$

E.

$$\begin{array}{r} 285 \\ -\ 63 \\ \hline \end{array}$$

If you have completed examples D and E, turn to page 58 to learn if you have identified George's error pattern correctly. What instructional procedures might you use to help George or any other student with this problem?

Error Pattern S-W-3

Donna gets many incorrect answers when she subtracts. Can you find a pattern of errors?

Name ___Donna___

A.
$$
\begin{array}{r}
147 \\
-\ 20 \\
\hline
120
\end{array}
$$

B.
$$
\begin{array}{r}
624 \\
-\ 323 \\
\hline
301
\end{array}
$$

C.
$$
\begin{array}{r}
527 \\
-\ 304 \\
\hline
203
\end{array}
$$

D.
$$
\begin{array}{r}
805 \\
-\ 201 \\
\hline
604
\end{array}
$$

Use Donna's error pattern to complete these examples.

E.
$$
\begin{array}{r}
446 \\
-\ 302 \\
\hline
\end{array}
$$

F.
$$
\begin{array}{r}
760 \\
-\ 230 \\
\hline
\end{array}
$$

After examples E and F are completed, turn to page 59 and see if you have actually found Donna's pattern of errors. What might have caused Donna to begin such a procedure?

Error Pattern S-W-4

Barbara seemed to be doing well with subtraction until recently. Can you find a pattern of errors in her work?

Name *Barbara*

A.
$$\begin{array}{r} \overset{8}{6}\overset{1}{9}3 \\ -248 \\ \hline 445 \end{array}$$

B.
$$\begin{array}{r} \overset{2}{3}\overset{1}{2}5 \\ -151 \\ \hline 174 \end{array}$$

C.
$$\begin{array}{r} \overset{5}{7}\overset{1}{2}\overset{1}{6} \\ -349 \\ \hline 287 \end{array}$$

D.
$$\begin{array}{r} \overset{2}{4}\overset{}{3}\overset{1}{4} \\ -276 \\ \hline 68 \end{array}$$

To make sure you have found the pattern, use Barbara's procedure to complete these examples.

E.
$$\begin{array}{r} 436 \\ -172 \\ \hline \end{array}$$

F.
$$\begin{array}{r} 625 \\ -348 \\ \hline \end{array}$$

After you complete examples E and F, turn to page 60 to see if you found Barbara's error pattern. What might have caused Barbara to begin using such a procedure?

Error Pattern S-W-5

Sam is having difficulty subtracting whole numbers. Do you find an erroneous pattern in his work?

Name ___Sam___

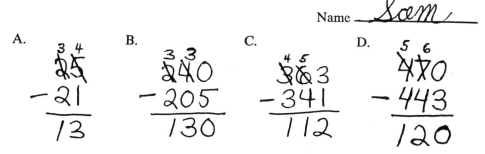

A.
```
  3 4
  2̸5̸
 -21
 ────
  13
```

B.
```
  3 3
  2̸4̸0
 -205
 ────
  130
```

C.
```
   4 5
   5̸6̸3
 -341
 ─────
  112
```

D.
```
   5 6
   4̸7̸0
 -443
 ─────
  120
```

In order to check your findings, use Sam's error pattern to compute examples E and F.

E.
```
  385
 -322
 ────
```

F.
```
  640
 -626
 ────
```

After you complete examples E and F, turn to page 61 to see if you found Sam's procedure. How would you help Sam or any child using such a procedure?

Error Pattern M-W-1

Examine Bob's written work carefully. What error pattern has he adopted?

Name ___Bob___

A.
$$\begin{array}{r} \overset{2}{4}6 \\ \times\ 24 \\ \hline 184 \\ 102 \\ \hline 1204 \end{array}$$

B.
$$\begin{array}{r} \overset{1}{7}6 \\ \times\ 32 \\ \hline 152 \\ 228 \\ \hline 2432 \end{array}$$

C.
$$\begin{array}{r} \overset{5}{4}8 \\ \times\ 57 \\ \hline 336 \\ 250 \\ \hline 2836 \end{array}$$

Were you able to identify Bob's error pattern? Check yourself by using the error pattern to compute examples D and E.

D.
$$\begin{array}{r} 98 \\ \times\ 56 \\ \hline \end{array}$$

E.
$$\begin{array}{r} 86 \\ \times\ 45 \\ \hline \end{array}$$

When you have completed examples D and E, turn to page 62 to see if you identified Bob's error pattern correctly. What instructional procedures might you use to help Bob or another student with this problem?

Error Pattern M-W-2

Many of Bill's answers are not correct. Can you find an error pattern?

Name _Bill_

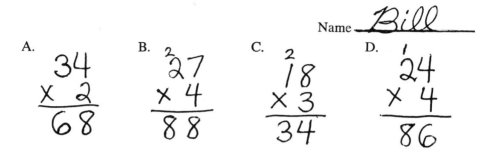

A.
$$\begin{array}{r} 34 \\ \times\ 2 \\ \hline 68 \end{array}$$

B.
$$\begin{array}{r} \overset{2}{2}7 \\ \times\ 4 \\ \hline 88 \end{array}$$

C.
$$\begin{array}{r} \overset{2}{1}8 \\ \times\ 3 \\ \hline 34 \end{array}$$

D.
$$\begin{array}{r} \overset{1}{2}4 \\ \times\ 4 \\ \hline 86 \end{array}$$

Check yourself by using the error pattern you have observed to complete examples E and F.

E.
$$\begin{array}{r} 35 \\ \times\ 3 \\ \hline \end{array}$$

F.
$$\begin{array}{r} 28 \\ \times\ 4 \\ \hline \end{array}$$

Turn to page 62 and see if you have correctly identified Bill's error pattern. How might you help Bill or other children who have adopted this procedure?

Error Pattern M-W-3

Joe's paper illustrates a common error pattern. Can you find it?

Name _Joe_

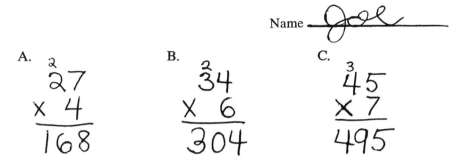

A.
```
  2
 27
x  4
────
168
```

B.
```
  2
 34
x  6
────
304
```

C.
```
  3
 45
x  7
────
495
```

When you think you have found Joe's error pattern, use his pattern to complete these examples.

D.
```
 68
x 5
───
```

E.
```
 29
x 3
───
```

After you have finished examples D and E, turn to page 63 to see if you have correctly identified Joe's error pattern. What could possibly have caused Joe to learn such a procedure?

Error Pattern M-W-4

Doug seems to multiply correctly by a one-digit multiplier, but he is having trouble with two- and three-digit multipliers. Can you find this error pattern?

Name — *Doug*

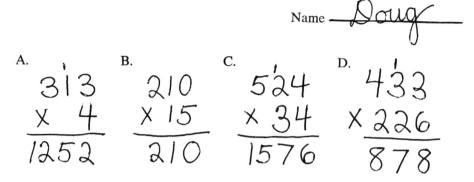

A.
$$\begin{array}{r} 3\overset{1}{1}3 \\ \times\ \ 4 \\ \hline 1252 \end{array}$$

B.
$$\begin{array}{r} 210 \\ \times\ 15 \\ \hline 210 \end{array}$$

C.
$$\begin{array}{r} 5\overset{1}{2}4 \\ \times\ 34 \\ \hline 1576 \end{array}$$

D.
$$\begin{array}{r} 4\overset{1}{3}3 \\ \times 226 \\ \hline 878 \end{array}$$

Did you find his pattern? Check yourself by using Doug's error pattern to complete examples E and F.

E.
$$\begin{array}{r} 621 \\ \times\ 23 \\ \hline \end{array}$$

F.
$$\begin{array}{r} 517 \\ \times 463 \\ \hline \end{array}$$

After examples E and F are completed, turn to page 64 to learn if you have correctly identified Doug's procedure. What remedial instruction might you initiate with Doug or any child using such a procedure?

Error Pattern D-W-1

Look very carefully at Jim's written work. What erroneous procedure has he used?

Name *Jim*

A.
$$\frac{233}{2\overline{)176}}$$

B.
$$\frac{221}{4\overline{)824}}$$

C.
$$\frac{231}{3\overline{)713}}$$

Did you find the erroneous procedure? Check yourself by using Jim's procedure to compute examples D and E.

D.
$$3\overline{)639}$$

E.
$$4\overline{)518}$$

After completing examples D and E, turn to pattern D-W-1 on page 65 and learn if you correctly identified Jim's error pattern. What instructional procedures might you use to help Jim or any other student using this procedure?

Error Pattern D-W-2

Look carefully at Gail's written work. Can you find the error pattern she has followed?

Name _Gail_

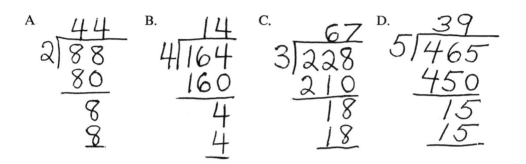

A.
$$\begin{array}{r} 44 \\ 2\overline{)88} \\ 80 \\ \hline 8 \\ 8 \\ \hline \end{array}$$

B.
$$\begin{array}{r} 14 \\ 4\overline{)164} \\ 160 \\ \hline 4 \\ 4 \\ \hline \end{array}$$

C.
$$\begin{array}{r} 67 \\ 3\overline{)228} \\ 210 \\ \hline 18 \\ 18 \\ \hline \end{array}$$

D.
$$\begin{array}{r} 39 \\ 5\overline{)465} \\ 450 \\ \hline 15 \\ 15 \\ \hline \end{array}$$

Did you find the incorrect procedure? Check yourself by using the error pattern to compute these examples.

E.
$$3\overline{)75}$$

F.
$$6\overline{)516}$$

Next turn to page 66 to see if you identified the error pattern correctly. Why might Gail or any child have adopted such an incorrect procedure?

Error Pattern D-W-3

John has been doing well with much of his work in division, but he is having difficulty now. Can you find his error pattern?

Name _John_

A.
$$\begin{array}{r} 65\,r1 \\ 7\overline{)456} \\ 42 \\ \hline 36 \\ 35 \\ \hline 1 \end{array}$$

B.
$$\begin{array}{r} 94\,r2 \\ 6\overline{)5426} \\ 54 \\ \hline 26 \\ 24 \\ \hline 2 \end{array}$$

C.
$$\begin{array}{r} 67\,r4 \\ 8\overline{)4860} \\ 48 \\ \hline 60 \\ 56 \\ \hline 4 \end{array}$$

D.
$$\begin{array}{r} 54\,r3 \\ 8\overline{)4035} \\ 40 \\ \hline 35 \\ 32 \\ \hline 3 \end{array}$$

Try John's procedure with these examples.

E.
$$9\overline{)2721}$$

F.
$$6\overline{)4250}$$

After you have completed examples E and F, turn to page 67 to learn if you have correctly identified John's error pattern. Why might John be using such a procedure?

Error Pattern D-W-4

Anita seems to have difficulty with some division problems but she solves other problems correctly. Can you find her pattern of error?

Name *Anita*

A.
$$5\overline{)254}^{50}R4$$
$$\underline{250}$$
$$4$$

B.
$$9\overline{)4560}^{560}R6$$
$$\underline{4500}$$
$$60$$
$$\underline{54}$$
$$6$$

C.
$$8\overline{)5840}^{730}$$
$$\underline{5600}$$
$$240$$
$$\underline{240}$$

D.
$$7\overline{)2149}^{370}$$
$$\underline{2100}$$
$$49$$
$$\underline{49}$$

Did you find Anita's procedure? Check yourself by using her pattern to complete these examples.

E.
$$6\overline{)4818}$$

F.
$$7\overline{)3525}$$

When examples E and F are completed, turn to page 68 and learn if you found Anita's error pattern. How might you help Anita or any other child using such a procedure?

Error Pattern E–F–1

Greg frequently makes errors when attempting to change a fraction to lower terms. What procedure is he using?

Name __Greg__

A. $\dfrac{19}{95} = \dfrac{1}{5}$

B. $\dfrac{13}{39} = \dfrac{1}{9}$

C. $\dfrac{18}{81} = \dfrac{1}{1}$

D. $\dfrac{12}{24} = \dfrac{1}{4}$

Determine if you have correctly identified Greg's error pattern by using his procedure to change examples E and F to lower terms.

E. $\dfrac{16}{64} =$

F. $\dfrac{14}{42}$

Now, turn to page 69 and see if you have identified the error pattern correctly. Why might Greg be using such an incorrect procedure?

Error Pattern E–F–2

Jill determined the simplest terms for each given fraction, some already in simplest terms and some not. What procedure did she use?

Name _Jill_

A.
$$\frac{4}{9} = \frac{2}{3}$$

B.
$$\frac{3}{9} = \frac{1}{3}$$

C.
$$\frac{3}{8} = \frac{1}{4}$$

D.
$$\frac{4}{8} = \frac{2}{4}$$

Find out if you have correctly identified Jill's procedure by using her error pattern to complete examples E and F.

E.
$$\frac{3}{4} =$$

F.
$$\frac{2}{8} =$$

Next, turn to page 69 where Jill's pattern is described. How might you help Jill or others using such a pattern?

Error Pattern E–F–3

Sue tried to change each fraction to lowest or simplest terms, but her results are quite unreasonable. Can you find her error pattern?

Name _Sue_

A. $\dfrac{4}{8} = \dfrac{2}{8}$ B. $\dfrac{6}{8} = \dfrac{1}{8}$ C. $\dfrac{2}{4} = \dfrac{2}{4}$

D. $\dfrac{7}{7} = \dfrac{1}{7}$ E. $\dfrac{4}{6} = \dfrac{1}{6}$ F. $\dfrac{9}{3} = \dfrac{3}{9}$

Use Sue's procedures with these fractions to learn if you have found her pattern.

G. $\dfrac{3}{6} =$ H. $\dfrac{6}{4} =$

After examples G and H are completed, turn to page 70 to see if you found Sue's error pattern. How would you help Sue or any child using such a procedure?

Error Pattern A–F–1

Can you find Robbie's pattern of error?

Name _Robbie_

A. $\dfrac{4}{5} + \dfrac{2}{3} = \dfrac{6}{8}$

B. $\dfrac{1}{4} + \dfrac{2}{3} = \dfrac{3}{7}$

C. $\dfrac{7}{8} + \dfrac{5}{6}$

D. $\dfrac{3}{7} + \dfrac{1}{2} = \dfrac{4}{9}$

Did you find the pattern? Make sure by using the pattern to compute these examples.

E. $\dfrac{3}{4} + \dfrac{1}{5} =$

F. $\dfrac{2}{3} + \dfrac{5}{6} =$

When you have completed examples E and F, turn to page 71 and see if you identified the pattern correctly. Why might Robbie be using such a procedure?

Error Pattern A–F–2

What error pattern has Dave adopted?

Name _Dave_

A.
$$6\tfrac{1}{2} = \tfrac{2}{4}$$
$$+\ 7\tfrac{1}{4} = \tfrac{1}{4}$$
$$\overline{\ \tfrac{3}{4}}$$

B.
$$10\tfrac{5}{6} = \tfrac{5}{6}$$
$$+\ 25\tfrac{2}{3} = \tfrac{4}{6}$$
$$\overline{\ \tfrac{9}{6} = 1\tfrac{1}{2}}$$

C.
$$24\tfrac{1}{2} = \tfrac{4}{8}$$
$$+\ 17\tfrac{5}{8} = \tfrac{5}{8}$$
$$\overline{\ \tfrac{9}{8} = 1\tfrac{1}{8}}$$

Did you find Dave's error pattern? Check yourself by using the error pattern to compute examples D and E.

D.
$$9\tfrac{1}{3}$$
$$+\ 5\tfrac{5}{9}$$

E.
$$16\tfrac{3}{4}$$
$$+\ 23\tfrac{1}{2}$$

When you complete examples D and E, turn to page 72 and see if you have identified Dave's error pattern correctly. What instructional procedures could you use to help Dave or another student using this error pattern?

Error Pattern A–F–3

Allen is having difficulty with addition of unlike fractions. Is there a pattern of errors in his work?

Name _Allen_

A.
$$\frac{1}{4} + \frac{2}{3} = \frac{6}{7} + \frac{4}{7} = \frac{10}{7}$$

B.
$$\frac{1}{3} + \frac{3}{5} = \frac{15}{8} + \frac{3}{8} = \frac{18}{8}$$

C.
$$\frac{2}{3} + \frac{1}{2} = \frac{2}{5} + \frac{6}{5} = \frac{8}{5}$$

To find out if you have identified Allen's error pattern, use his erroneous procedure to complete these examples.

D.
$$\frac{1}{4} + \frac{1}{5} =$$

E.
$$\frac{2}{5} + \frac{1}{2} =$$

When you have completed examples D and E, turn to page 73 and see if you have actually found Allen's pattern of errors. What might have caused Allen to begin using such a senseless procedure?

Error Pattern S–F–1

Andrew did fairly well with addition of fractions and mixed numbers, but he seems to be having trouble with subtraction. Can you find a pattern or patterns in his work?

Name *Andrew*

A.
$$7\tfrac{1}{2}$$
$$-3$$
$$\overline{4\tfrac{1}{2}}$$

B.
$$8\tfrac{1}{3}$$
$$-\tfrac{2}{3}$$
$$\overline{8\tfrac{1}{3}}$$

C.
$$6$$
$$-1\tfrac{1}{4}$$
$$\overline{5\tfrac{1}{4}}$$

D.
$$3\tfrac{1}{4}$$
$$-2\tfrac{3}{4}$$
$$\overline{1\tfrac{2}{4}}$$

Make sure you have found Andrew's pattern or patterns by using his procedures to complete these examples.

E.
$$5\tfrac{1}{5}$$
$$-3\tfrac{3}{5}$$

F.
$$1$$
$$-\tfrac{1}{3}$$

When you have completed examples E and F, turn to page 74 to see if you found Andrew's procedures. Why might Andrew be using such procedures?

Error Pattern S-F-2

Don is having difficulty with subtracting mixed numbers. Can you find his pattern of errors?

Name _Don_

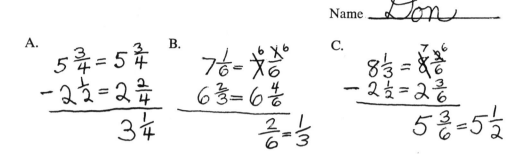

A.
$$5\tfrac{3}{4} = 5\tfrac{3}{4}$$
$$-2\tfrac{1}{2} = 2\tfrac{2}{4}$$
$$\overline{\qquad 3\tfrac{1}{4}}$$

B.
$$7\tfrac{1}{6} = \cancel{7}\tfrac{6\times6}{6}$$
$$6\tfrac{2}{3} = 6\tfrac{4}{6}$$
$$\overline{\qquad \tfrac{2}{6} = \tfrac{1}{3}}$$

C.
$$8\tfrac{1}{3} = \cancel{8}\tfrac{7\times6}{6}$$
$$-2\tfrac{1}{2} = 2\tfrac{3}{6}$$
$$\overline{\qquad 5\tfrac{3}{6} = 5\tfrac{1}{2}}$$

Did you find Don's procedure? Check yourself by using his procedure to complete these examples.

D.
$$6\tfrac{5}{8}$$
$$-3\tfrac{1}{4}$$

E.
$$4\tfrac{3}{8}$$
$$-1\tfrac{1}{2}$$

After you have completed examples E and F, turn to page 75 to see if you have found Don's error pattern. How might you help Don or any student using such a procedure?

Error Pattern S-F-3

Look carefully at Chuck's written work. What error pattern has he followed?

Name *Chuck*

A. $8\frac{3}{4} - 6\frac{1}{8} = 2\frac{2}{4}$

B. $5\frac{3}{8} - 2\frac{2}{3} = 3\frac{1}{5}$

C. $9\frac{1}{5} - 1\frac{3}{8} = 8\frac{2}{3}$

D. $7\frac{2}{5} - 4\frac{7}{10} = 3\frac{5}{5}$

If you found Chuck's error pattern, check yourself by using his procedure to compute these examples.

E. $6\frac{2}{3} - 3\frac{1}{6} =$

F. $4\frac{5}{8} - 1\frac{3}{4} =$

Now turn to page 76 to see if you identified the error pattern correctly. Why might a child use such a computational procedure?

Error Pattern M–F–1

Dan is having considerable difficulty. What error pattern is he following in his written work?

Name *Dan*

A. $\dfrac{4}{5} \times \dfrac{3}{4} = 166$ B. $\dfrac{1}{2} \times \dfrac{3}{8} = 68$

C. $\dfrac{2}{9} \times \dfrac{1}{5} = 100$ D. $\dfrac{2}{3} \times \dfrac{4}{6} = 132$

Use Dan's procedure for these examples to make sure you have found his error pattern.

E. $\dfrac{3}{4} \times \dfrac{2}{3} =$ F. $\dfrac{4}{9} \times \dfrac{2}{5} =$

When you have completed examples E and F, turn to page 76. Why might Dan be using such a procedure?

Error Pattern M–F–2

Grace gets many answers correct when computing with fractions, but she is having difficulty with multiplication examples. See if you can find her error pattern.

A.
$$\frac{3}{8} \times \frac{5}{6} = \frac{3}{8} \times \frac{6}{5} = \frac{18}{40}$$

Name _Grace_

B.
$$\frac{2}{5} \times \frac{3}{4} = \frac{2}{5} \times \frac{4}{3} = \frac{8}{15}$$

C.
$$\frac{4}{5} \times \frac{2}{3} = \frac{4}{5} \times \frac{3}{2} = \frac{12}{10}$$

Use Grace's procedure for the following examples to make sure you have found her error pattern.

D.
$$\frac{2}{3} \times \frac{3}{4} =$$

E.
$$\frac{5}{7} \times \frac{3}{8} =$$

When you have completed examples D and E, turn to page 77. Why might Grace be using such a procedure?

Error Pattern D–F–1

Linda has difficulty when she tries to divide with fractions. What procedure is she using?

Name *Linda*

A. $\frac{4}{6} \div \frac{2}{2} = \frac{2}{3}$

B. $\frac{6}{8} \div \frac{2}{8} = \frac{3}{1}$

C. $\frac{6}{10} \div \frac{2}{4} = \frac{3}{2}$

D. $\frac{7}{2} \div \frac{3}{5} = \frac{2}{2}$

Find out if you correctly identified Linda's procedure by using her error pattern to complete examples E and F.

E. $\frac{4}{12} \div \frac{4}{4} =$

F. $\frac{13}{20} \div \frac{5}{6} =$

Next, turn to page 78 where Linda's pattern is described. How might you help Linda and others using such a procedure?

Error Pattern A-D-1

Examine Harold's work carefully. Can you find the error pattern he is following?

Name _Harold_

A.
$$\begin{array}{r} .8 \\ +.4 \\ \hline .12 \end{array}$$

B.
$$\begin{array}{r} .6 \\ +.9 \\ \hline .15 \end{array}$$

C.
$$\begin{array}{r} .4 \\ +.3 \\ \hline .7 \end{array}$$

D.
$$\begin{array}{r} .5 \\ +.8 \\ \hline .13 \end{array}$$

Did you find the pattern? Check yourself by using his error pattern to compute these examples.

E.
$$\begin{array}{r} .3 \\ +.5 \\ \hline \end{array}$$

F.
$$\begin{array}{r} .7 \\ +.7 \\ \hline \end{array}$$

After you have completed examples E and F, turn to page 79 and verify your responses. What might have caused Harold to begin using such a procedure?

Error Pattern M–D–1

Marsha seems to have difficulty with some multiplication problems involving decimals but she solves other examples correctly. Can you find her pattern of error?

Name *Marsha*

A.
$$
\begin{array}{r}
6.45 \\
\times \quad 3 \\
\hline
19.35
\end{array}
$$

B.
$$
\begin{array}{r}
32.7 \\
\times \quad .5 \\
\hline
16.35
\end{array}
$$

C.
$$
\begin{array}{r}
21.8 \\
\times \quad .4 \\
\hline
87.2
\end{array}
$$

D.
$$
\begin{array}{r}
4.35 \\
\times \quad 2.3 \\
\hline
13\,05 \\
87\,0 \\
\hline
100.05
\end{array}
$$

Did you find Marsha's procedure? Check yourself by using her pattern to complete these examples.

E.
$$
\begin{array}{r}
405 \\
\times \quad .6 \\
\hline
\end{array}
$$

F.
$$
\begin{array}{r}
6.7 \\
\times \quad 3 \\
\hline
\end{array}
$$

When examples E and F are completed, turn to page 79 and learn if you found Marsha's error pattern. How might you help Marsha or any other child using such a procedure?

Error Pattern D–D–1

Ted frequently makes errors when dividing decimals. Can you find his procedure?

Name _Ted_

A.
$$
\begin{array}{r}
3.91 \\
6\overline{\smash{)}23.5} \\
18 \\
\hline
55 \\
54 \\
\hline
1
\end{array}
$$

B.
$$
\begin{array}{r}
9.62 \\
.4\overline{\smash{)}38.6} \\
36 \\
\hline
26 \\
24 \\
\hline
2
\end{array}
$$

C.
$$
\begin{array}{r}
1.644 \\
5\overline{\smash{)}8.24} \\
5 \\
\hline
32 \\
30 \\
\hline
24 \\
20 \\
\hline
4
\end{array}
$$

Use Ted's procedure with these examples to see if you have found his error pattern.

D. $3\overline{\smash{)}2.57}$ E. $7\overline{\smash{)}9.35}$

Now, turn to page 80 and see if you have identified the error pattern correctly. Why might Ted be using such an incorrect procedure?

Error Pattern S-M-1

Margaret is having difficulty with computation involving measurement. Can you find an error pattern in her work?

Name _Margaret_

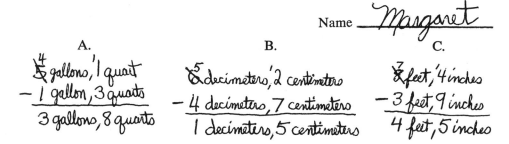

A.
4
5̶ gallons, 1 quart
− 1 gallon, 3 quarts
3 gallons, 8 quarts

B.
5
6̶ decimeters, 2 centimeters
− 4 decimeters, 7 centimeters
1 decimeters, 5 centimeters

C.
7
8̶ feet, 4 inches
− 3 feet, 9 inches
4 feet, 5 inches

Check yourself by using Margaret's erroneous pattern to complete these examples.

D.
6 yards, 1 foot
− 2 yards, 2 feet

E.
3 quarts, 1 cup
− 1 quart, 3 cups

After you have finished examples D and E, turn to page 81 to see if you have accurately identified Margaret's error pattern. Why might Margaret or any other child use such a procedure?

3

Analyzing Error Patterns
in Computation

In this chapter error patterns are described and analyzed. Accompanying many of the patterns is a discussion which focuses upon the question of why some children learn to compute with error patterns. In many cases an erroneous computational procedure sometimes produces the correct answer, thereby confirming the validity of the pattern in the mind of the child. Evidences of purely mechanical procedures will abound. Such procedures cannot be explained by the child through mathematical principles or with physical aids. Children who use mechanical procedures "push symbols around" whenever there are examples to be computed and right answers to be determined. Many of the children represented here have been introduced to the standard short-form algorithms too soon; some lack very basic understandings of the operations themselves; others have become careless and confused. Each child has practiced his or her erroneous procedure and uses the procedure regularly.

As you read about an error pattern you will have an opportunity to suggest corrective or remedial instruction. Remember, these boys and girls may be in your classroom soon. What will you do to help them? Many children who are having difficulty computing with whole numbers do not have an adequate understanding of numeration. You may want to take note of the suggestions in Appendix C before suggesting remedial activities.

Error Pattern A-W-1

used by Mike on page 20.

Using the error pattern, examples E and F would be computed as they appear below.

E.
$$43$$
$$+\ 65$$
$$\overline{108}$$

F.
$$88$$
$$+\ 39$$
$$\overline{1117}$$

If your responses are the same as these, you were able to identify Mike's erroneous computational procedure. The ones were added and recorded, then the tens were added and recorded (or vice versa). The sum of the ones and the sum of the tens were each recorded without regard to place value in the sum. Note that Mike may have applied some knowledge of place value in his work with the two addends, *i.e.,* he may have treated the 88 in example F as 8 tens and 8 ones, and his answer as 11 tens and 17 ones. It is also true that Mike may have merely thought "8 plus 9 equals 17, and 8 plus 3 equals 11." I have found many students who think through such a problem in this way; some of these students also emphasize that you add 8 and 9 first because "you add the ones first."

Mike has the idea of adding ones with ones — possibly from work with bundles of sticks and single sticks. He apparently knows he should consider all of the single sticks together. He *may* know a rule for exchanging or regrouping ten single sticks for one bundle of ten, but, if he does, he has not applied the rule to these examples. Previous instruction may not have given adequate emphasis to the mechanics of recording sums.

If you were Mike's teacher, what remedial steps might you take? Describe two instructional activities which would hopefully correct the error pattern.

1. _____

_____

_____

2. _____

_____

_____

When you have completed your responses, turn to page 84 to see if your suggestions are among the alternatives described.

Error Pattern A-W-2

from Mary's paper on page 21.

If you used Mary's error pattern, you completed examples E and F as they are shown below.

E.

$$254$$
$$+\ 535$$
$$\overline{789}$$

F.

$$6\overset{3}{1}\overset{2}{8}$$
$$+\ 782$$
$$\overline{1112}$$

This pattern is a reversal of the procedure used in the usual algorithm—without regard for place value. Addition is performed from left to right, and, when the sum of a column is ten or greater, the left figure is recorded and the right figure is placed above the next column to the right.

You probably noted that example A on page 21 and example E above are correct. In these two examples, Mary's use of a left-to-right procedure was reinforced, for she computed the correct sum. In such cases, use of an erroneous procedure is very apt to go unnoticed by the classroom teacher; yet the erroneous pattern, or at least part of it, is practiced and "mastered."

If you were Mary's teacher, what corrective procedures might you follow? Describe two instructional activities which would hopefully help Mary add correctly.

1. _____

_____

_____

2. _____

_____

_____

When your responses are complete, turn to page 85 and see if your suggestions are among the alternatives described.

Error Pattern A-W-3

from Carol's paper on page 22.

If you found Carol's error pattern, your results are the same as the erroneous computation shown below.

F.	G.	H.
26	60	74
+ 3	+ 24	+ 5
——	——	——
11	84	16

Carol misses examples in which one of the addends is written as a single digit. When working such examples, she adds the three digits as if they were all units. When both addends are two-digit numbers, she appears to add correctly. However, it is quite probable that Carol is not applying any knowledge of place value with either type of example. She may be merely adding units in every case. (When both addends are two-digit numbers, she adds units in straight columns. When one addend is a one-digit number, she adds the three digits along a curve.) If this is the way Carol is thinking, she will probably experience even more failure and frustration when she begins addition and subtraction requiring regrouping.

Carol needs help. How would you help her? Describe at least two instructional activities you believe would correct Carol's error pattern.

1. _____

_____

_____

2. _____

_____

_____

After you have described at least two activities, turn to page 86 and compare your suggestions with the suggestions listed there.

Error Pattern A-W-4

from Dorothy's paper on page 23.

Using Dorothy's error pattern, examples E and F would be computed as they appear below.

E.
$$\overset{\scriptscriptstyle 1}{46} \\ +\ \underline{8} \\ 134$$

F.
$$\overset{\scriptscriptstyle 1}{98} \\ +\ \underline{3} \\ 131$$

Dorothy is not having difficulty with her basic addition facts, but higher decade addition situations are confusing her. She tries to use the regular addition algorithm; however, when she adds the tens column she adds in the one-digit number again.

If Dorothy has been introduced to the multiplication algorithm, she may persist in seeing similar patterns for computation whenever numerals are arranged as she has seen them in multiplication examples. Changing operations when the arrangement of numerals is similar is difficult for some children. An interview with Dorothy may help you determine if she really knows how to add problems like these. When working with a child who tends to carry over one situation into his perception of another, avoid extensive practice at a given time on any single procedure.

How would you help Dorothy? Describe at least two instructional activities which would help Dorothy replace her erroneous pattern with a correct procedure.

1. _____

_____

_____

2. _____

_____

_____

When both activities are described, turn to page 87 and compare your suggestions with the suggestions recorded there.

Error Pattern S-W-1

from Cheryl's paper on page 24.

Using the error pattern, examples E and F would be computed as they appear below.

E.
$$458 \\ -\ \underline{372} \\ 126$$

F.
$$241 \\ -\ \underline{96} \\ 255$$

Did you identify the error pattern? As a general rule, the ones are subtracted and recorded, then the tens are subtracted and recorded, etc. Apparently Cheryl is considering each position (ones, tens, etc.) as a separate subtraction problem. In example E she probably did not think of the numbers 458 and 372, but only of 8 and 2, 5 and 7, and 4 and 3. Further, in subtracting single-digit numbers, she does not conceive of the upper figure (minuend) as the number in a set and the lower figure (subtrahend) as the number in a subset. When subtracting ones Cheryl may think of the larger of the two numbers as the number of the set, and the smaller as the number to be removed from the set. Or she may merely compare the two single-digit numbers much as she would match sets one to one or place rods side by side to find a difference. In example F she would think "1 and 6, the difference is 5." She uses the same procedure when subtracting tens and hundreds.

Note that example A on page 24 is correct. This example includes much smaller numbers than the other examples. It may be that Cheryl counted from 16 to 32, or she may have used some kind of number line. If she did think of 32 as "20 plus 12" in order to subtract, it may be the case that she applies renaming procedures only to smaller numbers which she can somehow conceptualize, but she breaks up larger numbers in the manner described above.

If you were Cheryl's teacher, what remedial steps might you take? Describe two instructional activities which would hopefully help Cheryl correct the error pattern.

1. _____

_____

_____

2. _____

_____

_____

After you have finished writing your responses, turn to page 88 to see if your suggestions are among the alternatives described.

Error Pattern S-W-2

from George's paper on page 25.

Did you identify the error pattern George used?

D.
$$\begin{array}{r} 2\overset{6}{\cancel{7}}\overset{i}{3} \\ -\ 38 \\ \hline 235 \end{array}$$

E.
$$\begin{array}{r} 2\overset{7}{\cancel{8}}\overset{/}{5} \\ -\ 63 \\ \hline 2112 \end{array}$$

George has learned to borrow or regroup in subtraction. In fact he regroups whether he needs to or not. It is possible that George would be able to interpret regrouping in terms of renaming a 10 as 10 ones, and it is also possible that he could interpret the answer (in example E) as 12 ones, 1 ten, and 2 hundreds. At any rate, his final answer does not take account of conventional place value notation.

You have no doubt observed that the answer to example D is correct. George's procedure is correct paper-and-pencil procedure for a problem such as example D. However, George does not distinguish between problems in which regrouping is required and problems which do not require regrouping; the fact that some of his answers are correct may positively reinforce the pattern he is using as appropriate for all subtraction problems.

George has a problem. How would you help him? Describe two instructional activities which would help George replace his error pattern with a correct computational procedure.

1. _____

_____

_____

2. _____

_____

_____

After you complete your two descriptions, turn to page 89 and compare what you have written with the suggestions presented there.

Error Pattern S-W-3

from Donna's paper, page 26.

Did you find Donna's error pattern?

E.
$$
\begin{array}{r}
446 \\
-302 \\
\hline
104
\end{array}
$$

F.
$$
\begin{array}{r}
760 \\
-230 \\
\hline
530
\end{array}
$$

Although Donna uses the subtraction fact $0 - 0 = 0$ correctly, she consistently writes "0" for the missing addend whenever the known addend (subtrahend) is zero. She regularly misses nine of the 100 basic subtraction facts because of this one difficulty.

We ought to be able to help Donna with a problem of this sort. How would you help her? Describe two instructional activities you think would enable Donna to subtract correctly.

1. _____

_____

_____

2. _____

_____

_____

Did you describe at least two activities? (It is important to have more than one possible instructional procedure in mind when working remedially with a child.) If so, turn to page 90 and compare your suggestions with the suggestions described there.

Error Pattern S-W-4

from Barbara's paper on page 27.

Did you find Barbara's error pattern?

E.
$$\begin{array}{r} \overset{3}{\cancel{4}}\overset{1}{3}6 \\ -\ 172 \\ \hline 264 \end{array}$$

F.
$$\begin{array}{r} \overset{4}{\cancel{6}}\overset{1}{2}\overset{1}{5} \\ -\ 348 \\ \hline 187 \end{array}$$

Barbara appeared to be doing well with subtraction until recently, when regrouping or renaming more than once was introduced. She apparently had been thinking something like "Take 1 from 4 and put the 1 in front of the 3" (example E). Now she has extended this procedure so that, in example F, she thinks, "In order to subtract (*i.e.,* in order to use a simple subtraction fact), I need a 1 in front of the 5 and a 1 in front of the 2. Take *two* 1's from the 6 . . . ." Note that if Barbara had not been showing her work with crutches of some sort, it would have been much more difficult to find the pattern.

Help is needed, and promptly—before she reinforces her error pattern with further practice. How would you help her? Describe two instructional activities you think would make it possible for Barbara to subtract correctly, even in examples such as these.

1. _____

_____

_____

2. _____

_____

_____

When you have described two instructional activities, turn to page 92 and compare your suggestions with the suggestions listed there.

Error Pattern S-W-5

from Sam's paper on page 28.

Did you find Sam's error pattern?

$$
\begin{array}{cc}
\text{E.} & \overset{4\;\;7}{\cancel{8}\cancel{8}5} \\
- & 322 \\
\hline
& 153
\end{array}
\qquad
\begin{array}{cc}
\text{F.} & \overset{7\;\;3}{\cancel{8}\cancel{4}0} \\
- & 626 \\
\hline
& 110
\end{array}
$$

Whenever the digits in the minuend and the subtrahend are the same, Sam borrows "so he will be able to subtract." However, his procedure is simply "Take one from here and add it here." It is not meaningful regrouping. You may also have noted that Sam has difficulty with zeros in the minuend. Rather than regrouping so he can subtract, he merely records a zero.

How would you help Sam if you had the opportunity? Describe at least two instructional activities which you believe would help Sam subtract whole numbers correctly.

1. _____

_____

_____

2. _____

_____

_____

After you have written both descriptions, turn to page 93 and see if your suggestions are among the suggestions listed there.

Error Pattern M-W-1

used by Bob on page 29.

Did you find the error pattern Bob used?

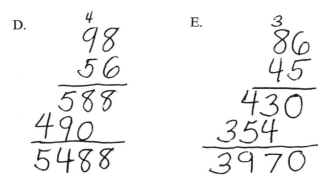

D.
$$\begin{array}{r} 4 \\ 98 \\ 56 \\ \hline 588 \\ 490 \\ \hline 5488 \end{array}$$

E.
$$\begin{array}{r} 3 \\ 86 \\ 45 \\ \hline 430 \\ 354 \\ \hline 3970 \end{array}$$

Consider example E. When multiplying 5 ones times 6 ones, Bob recorded the 3 tens as a crutch above the 8 tens to remind him to add 3 tens to the product of 5 and 8 tens. However, the crutch recorded when multiplying by ones was *also* used when multiplying by tens.

Note that the answers to example B on page 29 and example D above are correct. Bob's error pattern may have gone undetected because he gets enough correct answers, enough positive reinforcement, to convince him that he is using a correct procedure. There may have been enough correct answers to cause Bob's busy teacher to conclude that Bob was merely careless. But Bob *is* consistently applying an erroneous procedure.

How would you help Bob with his problem? Describe two instructional activities which would help Bob replace this error pattern with a correct computational procedure.

1. _____

_____

_____

2. _____

_____

_____

When you have written descriptions of two instructional activities, turn to page 94 and compare what you have written with the suggestions presented there.

Error Pattern M-W-2

from Bill's paper on page 30.

The examples below illustrate Bill's error pattern.

E.
$$
\begin{array}{r}
\overset{\scriptstyle 1}{35} \\
\times\ 3 \\
\hline
95
\end{array}
$$

F.
$$
\begin{array}{r}
\overset{\scriptstyle 3}{28} \\
\times\ 4 \\
\hline
82
\end{array}
$$

Bill simply does not add the number of tens he records with a crutch. Perhaps he knows he should add, but don't be too sure. He forgets consistently!

You ought to be able to help Bill with a problem of this sort. How would you help him? Describe two activities you think would enable Bill to complete the multiplication correctly.

1. _____

_____

_____

2. _____

_____

_____

Are both activities described? Then turn to page 96 and compare what you have written with the suggestions listed there.

Error Pattern M-W-3

from Joe's paper on page 31.

Did you find the error pattern Joe uses?

D.
$$
\begin{array}{r}
\overset{\scriptstyle 4}{68} \\
\times\ 5 \\
\hline
500
\end{array}
$$

E.
$$
\begin{array}{r}
\overset{\scriptstyle 2}{29} \\
\times\ 3 \\
\hline
127
\end{array}
$$

Joe is using an erroneous procedure which is all too frequently adopted by children. He adds the number associated with the crutch *before* multiplying the tens figure, whereas the algorithm requires that the tens figure be multiplied first. In example D, he thought "6 plus 4 equals 10 and 5 times 10 equals 50" instead of "5 times 6 equals 30 and 30 plus 4 equals 34." It may be that when Joe learned the addition algorithm involving regrouping, his teacher reminded him repeatedly, "The first thing you do is to add the number you carry." Many teachers drill children on such a rule, and it is little wonder that children sometimes apply the rule in inappropriate contexts.

The fact that children frequently use Joe's procedure does not lessen your obligation to help Joe multiply correctly. How would *you* help him? Describe two different instructional activities you think would enable Joe to replace his error pattern with a correct computational procedure.

1. _____

_____

_____

2. _____

_____

_____

When you have finished writing both descriptions, turn to page 98 and compare what you have written with the suggestions offered there.

Error Pattern M-W-4

from Doug's paper on page 32.

Did you find Doug's error pattern? If so, you completed examples E and F as they are shown below.

E.
$$\begin{array}{r} 621 \\ \times\ 23 \\ \hline 1243 \end{array}$$

F.
$$\begin{array}{r} 5\overset{2}{1}7 \\ \times\ 463 \\ \hline 2081 \end{array}$$

The procedure used by Doug is a blend of the algorithm for multiplying by a one-digit multiplier and the conventional addition algorithm. Each column is approached as a separate multiplication; when the multiplicand has more digits than the multiplier, the left-most digit of the multiplier continues to be used.

You may meet Doug in your own classroom. How would you help him? Describe at least two instructional activities you believe would enable Doug to multiply by two- and three-digit numbers correctly.

1. _____

_____

_____

2. _____

_____

_____

After your descriptions are written, turn to page 99 and see if your suggestions are among the suggestions listed there.

Error Pattern D-W-1

used by Jim on page 33.

Did you find the erroneous procedure Jim used?

D. 3)639 = 213   E. 4)518 = 142

Example D is correct and it does not give many clues to Jim's thinking. However, the fact that example D *is* correct is a reminder that erroneous procedures sometimes produce correct answers, thereby reinforcing the procedure as far as the student is concerned and making the error pattern more difficult for the teacher to identify.

Example E illustrates Jim's thinking more completely. Apparently Jim ignores place value in the dividend and quotient, and he thinks of each digit as "ones." Furthermore, he considers one digit of the dividend and the one-digit divisor as two numbers "to be divided." The larger of the two (whether the divisor or a digit within the dividend) is divided by the smaller and the result recorded. Interestingly, the remainder is ignored.

Did you notice that no numerals were recorded below the dividend? This lack in itself is a sign of possible trouble. It may well be that someone (a teacher, a parent, a friend) tried to teach Jim the "short" division procedure.

How would you help Jim with his problem? Describe two instructional activities which you think would help Jim replace this erroneous procedure with a correct computational procedure.

1. _____

_____

_____

2. _____

_____

_____

After you have written descriptions of two appropriate instructional activities, compare your activities with the suggestions on page 100.

Error Pattern D-W-2

from Gail's paper on page 34.

Using Gail's incorrect procedure, examples E and F would be computed as shown below.

E.
$$
\begin{array}{r}
52 \\
3\overline{\smash{)}75} \\
60 \\
\hline
15 \\
15 \\
\hline
\end{array}
$$

F.
$$
\begin{array}{r}
68 \\
6\overline{\smash{)}516} \\
480 \\
\hline
36 \\
36 \\
\hline
\end{array}
$$

Did you find the error pattern? In the ones column Gail records the first quotient figure she determines, and in the tens column she records the second digit she determines. In other words, the answer is recorded right to left. In the usual algorithms for addition, subtraction, and multiplication of whole numbers, the answer is recorded right to left; perhaps Gail assumes it is appropriate to do the same with the division algorithm.

The fact that example A is correct illustrates again that correct answers are sometimes obtained with incorrect procedures, thereby positively reinforcing an error pattern.

It is quite probable that, for example E, Gail thinks "7 divided by 3" (or perhaps "3 times what number is 7") rather than "70 divided by 3." The quotient for a short cut expression such as "7 divided by 3" would indeed be 2 units. Shortcuts in thinking and the standard algorithm for division may have been introduced too soon.

What would you do if you were Gail's teacher? What corrective steps might you take? Describe two instructional activities which you believe would help Gail correct the erroneous procedure.

1. _____

_____

_____

2. _____

_____

_____

If you have finished your responses, turn to page 102 and see if your suggestions are among the alternatives listed there.

Error Pattern D-W-3

from John's paper on page 35.

If you found John's error pattern, you completed examples E and F as they are shown below.

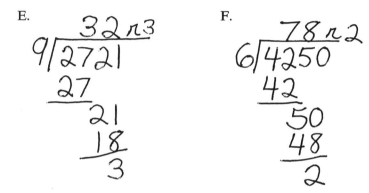

John is missing examples which include a zero in the tens place of the quotient. Whenever he brings down and cannot divide he brings down again, but without recording a zero to show that there are no tens. Careless placement of figures in the quotient may contribute to John's problem.

How would you help John? Describe at least two instructional activities you believe would help John correct his pattern of error.

1. _____

_____

_____

2. _____

_____

_____

When you have completed both descriptions, turn to page 103 and compare your suggestions with the suggestions listed there.

Error Pattern D-W-4

from Anita's paper on page 36.

If Anita's procedure is used, examples E and F would be completed as shown.

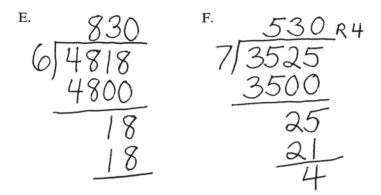

E.

$$\begin{array}{r} 830 \\ 6\overline{)4818} \\ 4800 \\ \hline 18 \\ 18 \\ \hline \end{array}$$

F.

$$\begin{array}{r} 530 \ R4 \\ 7\overline{)3525} \\ 3500 \\ \hline 25 \\ 21 \\ \hline 4 \end{array}$$

Like John, Anita is having difficulty with examples which include a zero in the tens place of the quotient. If she "brings down" and cannot divide, she "brings down" again; but she does not record a zero to show that there are no tens. However, she is careful to align her work in columns of hundreds, tens, etc., so that the quotient is obviously incomplete as she finishes her computation. Therefore, a zero is inserted in the remaining position—the ones place.

The extensive use of zeros in the computation (*e.g.,* the 4800 in example E) sometimes helps a child if the child consciously multiplies in terms of the total values involved. In example E, 800 × 6 = 4800. However, Anita also indicated that 30 × 6 = 18, which is not true. It may be the case that zeros are being written all the way across just because it is the thing to do. An interview with Anita, letting her think out loud while computing, may be helpful in determining what is actually happening.

What would *you* do to help Anita? Describe at least two instructional activities you believe would help her correct the pattern of error.

1. _____

_____

_____

2. _____

_____

_____

When both activities have been described, turn to page 104 and compare your suggestions with the suggestions recorded there.

Error Pattern E–F–1

from Greg's paper on page 37.

If Greg's procedure is used, examples E and F would be completed as follows:

E. $\dfrac{16}{64} = \dfrac{1}{4}$ F. $\dfrac{14}{42} = \dfrac{1}{2}$

If the same digit appears in both numerator and denominator, Greg uses a cancellation procedure similar to what he has apparently learned to apply whenever both expressions are written as products of two numbers. Though the procedure is erroneous, examples A and E are both correct, and Greg may find it difficult to believe his method is not satisfactory.

We ought to be able to help Greg. How would you help him? Describe two instructional activities you believe would help Greg correct his pattern of error.

1._____

_____

_____

2._____

_____

_____

After two activities have been described, turn to page 106 and compare what you have written with the suggestions listed there.

Error Pattern E-F-2

from Jill's paper on page 38.

Did you find Jill's error pattern?

E. $\dfrac{3}{4} = \dfrac{1}{2}$ F. $\dfrac{2}{8} = \dfrac{1}{4}$

Jill's computation appears almost random though, interestingly, several answers are correct. She obviously does not recognize which fractions are already in simplest terms. She explains her procedure as follows:

"4 goes to 2, and 9 goes to 3"
"3 goes to 1, and 9 goes to 3"

For examples E and F,

> "3 goes to 1, and 4 goes to 2"
> "2 goes to 1, and 8 goes to 4"

Jill simply associates a specific whole number with each given numerator or denominator. *All* 3's become 1's and *all* 4's become 2's when fractions are to be reduced or changed to simplest terms. This procedure is a very mechanical one, requiring no concept of a fraction; however, it does produce correct answers part of the time.

Jill has a very real problem. How would you help her? Describe two instructional activities which would help Jill replace this erroneous procedure with a correct procedure.

1. _____

_____

_____

2. _____

_____

_____

After two activities have been described, turn to page 106 and compare what you have written with the suggestions listed there.

Error Pattern E-F-3

from Sue's paper on page 39.

Did you correctly identify Sue's pattern of error? Many teachers would assume she had responded randomly.

G. $\dfrac{3}{6} = \dfrac{2}{6}$ H. $\dfrac{6}{4} = \dfrac{1}{6}$

Sue considers the given numerator and denominator as two whole numbers, and divides the larger by the smaller to determine the new numerator (ignoring any remainder); then the largest of the two numbers is copied as the new denominator. Perhaps she has observed that the denominator is usually the larger of the two numbers in the fractions she sees.

How would you help Sue? She is not unlike many other children who develop mechanistic and unreasonable procedures in arithmetic classes. Describe at least two instructional activities which you believe would help Sue learn to correctly change fractions to lowest or simplest terms.

1. _____

_____

_____

2. _____

_____

_____

When you have described at least two activities, turn to page 108 and compare your suggestions with the suggestions listed there.

Error Pattern A–F–1

from Robbie's paper on page 40.

Did you find Robbie's error pattern?

E. $\dfrac{3}{4} + \dfrac{1}{5} = \dfrac{4}{9}$ F. $\dfrac{2}{3} + \dfrac{5}{6} = \dfrac{7}{9}$

Robbie adds the numerators to get the numerator for the sum, then he adds the denominators to get the denominator for the sum. Lankford, in the research described in Chapter 1, found this procedure to be a "most prevalent practice."[1] It is likely that Robbie has already learned to multiply fractions, and he appears to be following a similar procedure for adding fractions.

Robbie has a problem. How would you help him? Describe two instructional activities which would help Robbie replace his error pattern with a correct computational procedure.

1._____

_____

_____

[1]Lankford, 1972, p. 30.

2._____

_____

_____

After you complete your two descriptions, turn to page 109 and compare what you have written with the suggestions presented there.

Error Pattern A-F-2

from Dave's paper on page 41.

Did you find the error pattern Dave is using?

D.
$$9\tfrac{1}{3} = \tfrac{3}{9}$$
$$+5\tfrac{5}{9} = \tfrac{5}{9}$$
$$\tfrac{8}{9}$$

E.
$$16\tfrac{3}{4} = \tfrac{3}{4}$$
$$+23\tfrac{1}{2} = \tfrac{2}{4}$$
$$\tfrac{5}{4} = 1\tfrac{1}{4}$$

Dave apparently becomes so involved with the process of renaming fractions that he forgets to add the whole numbers. He has probably been taught the following algorithm or one similar to it.

F.
$$9\tfrac{1}{3} = 9\tfrac{3}{9}$$
$$+5\tfrac{5}{9} = 5\tfrac{5}{9}$$
$$14\tfrac{8}{9}$$

G.
$$16\tfrac{3}{4} = 16\tfrac{3}{4}$$
$$+23\tfrac{1}{2} = 23\tfrac{2}{4}$$
$$39\tfrac{5}{4} = 40\tfrac{1}{4}$$

In the algorithm shown with examples F and G, required rewriting of mixed numerals sometimes results in carelessness on the part of children. They all too frequently write incorrect statements such as

$$9\tfrac{1}{3} = \tfrac{3}{9}$$

and

$$16\tfrac{3}{4} = \tfrac{3}{4}$$

How would you help Dave with his problem? Describe two instructional activities which you think would help Dave replace his error pattern with a correct computational procedure.

1. _____

_____

_____

2. _____

_____

_____

When you have finished describing both instructional activities, turn to page 110 and compare your suggestions with those listed there.

Error Pattern A-F-3

from Allen's paper on page 42.

Did you find Allen's error pattern?

D.
$$\frac{1}{4} + \frac{1}{5} = \frac{5}{9} + \frac{4}{9} = \frac{9}{9}$$

E.
$$\frac{2}{5} + \frac{1}{2} = \frac{2}{7} + \frac{10}{7} = \frac{12}{7}$$

Allen has learned a very mechanical procedure for changing two fractions so they will have the same denominator. Someone may have tried to teach him a rather common shortcut which includes rules for adding and multiplying different numerators in an apparently arbitrary pattern. However, what Allen actually learned was a very different pattern of additions and multiplications, a mechanical procedure he uses to "get an answer" when required to do so by a teacher. He first adds the unlike denominators to get a common denominator, then he multiplies the numerator and denominator of one fraction to get the numerator of the other fraction. (Apparently, he adds like fractions correctly.) If Allen has been practicing addition of unlike fractions, it is this erroneous procedure he has been reinforcing.

Can we help Allen with a problem of this sort? How would you help him? Describe at least two instructional activities you think would enable Allen to add unlike fractions correctly.

1. _____

_____

_____

2. _____

_____

_____

Have you described at least two activities? Remember, it is important to have more than one possible instructional procedure in mind when working remedially with a child. If so, turn to page 110 and compare your suggestions with the suggestions noted there.

Error Pattern S-F-1

from Andrew's paper on page 43.

Did you find Andrew's error patterns?

E.
$$5\frac{1}{5}$$
$$-\ 3\frac{3}{5}$$
$$2\frac{2}{5}$$

F.
$$1$$
$$-\ \frac{1}{3}$$
$$1\frac{1}{3}$$

In every case the whole numbers are subtracted as simple subtraction problems, perhaps even before attention is given to the column of common fractions. Where only one fraction appears in the problem (examples A and C) the fraction is simply "brought down." If two fractions appear, Andrew records the difference between them, ignoring whether the subtrahend or the minuend is the larger of the two.

How would you help Andrew? (You may want to review Error Pattern S-W-1 for ideas.) Describe two instructional activities you think would help Andrew correct his erroneous procedures.

1. _____

_____

_____

2. _____

_____

_____

When both descriptions are completed, turn to page 112 and compare your suggestions with the suggestions listed there.

Error Pattern S-F-2

from Don's paper on page 44.

If Don's procedure is used, examples D and E would be completed as they are shown below.

D.

$$6\frac{5}{8} = 6\frac{5}{8}$$
$$-\ 3\frac{1}{4} = 3\frac{2}{8}$$
$$3\frac{3}{8}$$

E.

$$4\frac{3}{8} = \cancel{4}\ \overset{3}{}\ \cancel{\frac{3}{8}}^{8}$$
$$-\ 1\frac{1}{2} = 1\frac{4}{8}$$
$$2\frac{4}{8} = 2\frac{1}{2}$$

Don appears to be able to subtract mixed numbers whenever no regrouping is necessary, and renaming fractions to higher and lower terms does not appear to be a problem for him. However, when renaming a mixed number in order to subtract, Don subtracts one whole or unit without properly adding an equivalent amount to the fraction. In every case, the numerator of the fraction is crossed out and the same number as the denominator is written in place of the numerator (rather than being added to the numerator). This may be, in part, confusion with the form of the unit (*i.e.,* $\frac{n}{n}$) which should be added to the existing fraction.

What would you do to help Don? Describe at least two instructional activities you believe would help him correct his pattern of errors.

1. _____

_____

_____

2. _____

_____

_____

When both activities have been described, turn to page 113 and compare your suggestions with the suggestions listed there.

Error Pattern S–F–3

from Chuck's paper on page 45.

Did you find Chuck's error pattern?

E. $6\frac{2}{3} - 3\frac{1}{6} = 3\frac{1}{3}$ F. $4\frac{5}{8} - 1\frac{3}{4} = 3\frac{3}{4}$

Chuck is subtracting by first finding the difference between the two whole numbers and recording that difference as the new whole number. He then finds the difference between the two numerators and records that difference as the new numerator. Finally, he finds the difference between the two denominators and records that number as the new denominator. The procedure is similar to addition as seen in Error Pattern A-F-1. However, children using this procedure for subtraction necessarily ignore the order of the minuend and the subtrahend.

Someone needs to come to Chuck's aid. How would you help him? Describe two instructional procedures you believe would help Chuck subtract correctly when given examples such as these.

1._____

_____

_____

2._____

_____

_____

When you have described two instructional activities, turn to page 114 and compare your suggestions with the suggestions listed there.

Error Pattern M–F–1

from Dan's paper on page 46.

Did you find Dan's error pattern?

E. $\frac{3}{4} \times \frac{2}{3} = 89$ F. $\frac{4}{9} \times \frac{2}{5} = 200$

Dan begins by multiplying the first numerator and the second denominator and recording the units digit of this product. If there is a tens digit, he remembers it to add later (as in multiplication of whole numbers). He then multiplies the first denominator and the second numerator, adds the number of tens remembered, and records this as the number of tens in the answer. The procedure involves a sort of cross multiplication and the multiply-then-add sequence from multiplication of whole numbers.

Dan uses this error pattern consistently; he has somehow learned to multiply fractions this way. How would you help him learn the correct procedure? Describe two instructional activities you believe would help.

1._____

_____

_____

2._____

_____

_____

After two activities have been described, turn to page 114 and compare what you have written with the suggestions listed there.

Error Pattern M-F-2

from Grace's paper on page 47.

Did you identify the error pattern Grace is using?

D. $\dfrac{2}{3} \times \dfrac{3}{4} = \dfrac{2}{3} \times \dfrac{4}{3} = \dfrac{8}{9}$

E. $\dfrac{5}{7} \times \dfrac{3}{8} = \dfrac{5}{7} \times \dfrac{8}{3} = \dfrac{40}{21}$

Grace has learned to invert and multiply, and she is using this division procedure to multiply fractions.

How would you help Grace? Describe two instructional activities which would help her replace this error pattern with the correct computational procedure.

1._____

_____

_____

2._____

_____

_____

After you complete your two descriptions, turn to page 115 and compare what you have written with the suggestions recorded there.

Error Pattern D–F–1

from Linda's paper on page 48.

Did you find the error pattern Linda is using?

E. $\dfrac{4}{12} \div \dfrac{4}{4} = \dfrac{1}{3}$ F. $\dfrac{13}{20} \div \dfrac{5}{6} = \dfrac{2}{3}$

Linda divides the first numerator by the second numerator and records the result as the numerator for the answer. She then determines the denominator for the answer by dividing the first denominator by the second denominator. In both divisions she ignores remainders. Note that examples A, B, and E are correct. It may be that she learned her procedure while the class was working with such examples. The common denominator method of dividing fractions may be part of the background, for her procedure is similar; however, she fails to change the fractions to equivalent fractions with the same denominator before dividing.

This is a tricky error pattern, producing both correct answers and absurd answers with zero numerators and denominators. Linda obviously needs help. How would you help her? Describe two instructional activities you think would enable her to replace her error pattern with a correct computational procedure.

1._____

_____

_____

2._____

_____

_____

When you have noted your descriptions, turn to page 116 and compare them with the suggestions listed there.

Error Pattern A-D-1

from Harold's paper on page 49.

Did you find Harold's error pattern?

E.

$$+\begin{array}{r} .3 \\ .5 \\ \hline .8 \end{array}$$

F.

$$+\begin{array}{r} .7 \\ .7 \\ \hline .14 \end{array}$$

Harold seemingly adds these decimal fractions as he would add whole numbers. The placement of the decimal point in the sum is a problem, but in every case he merely places the decimal point at the left of the sum.

We ought to be able to help Harold with a problem of this sort. How would *you* help him? Describe at least two instructional activities you believe would enable Harold to add such examples correctly.

1. ———————————————————————————

———————————————————————————

———————————————————————————

2. ———————————————————————————

—————————————————— ——————————

———————————————————————————

After you have recorded both activities, turn to page 117 and compare your suggestions with the suggestions listed there.

Error Pattern M–D–1

from Marsha's paper on page 50.

If you used Marsha's error pattern, you completed examples E and F as they are shown below.

E.

$$\begin{array}{r} 40.5 \\ \times\ .6 \\ \hline 24.30 \end{array}$$

F.

$$\begin{array}{r} 6.7 \\ \times\ 3 \\ \hline 2.01 \end{array}$$

In her answer, Marsha places the decimal point by counting over from the left instead of from the right. She frequently gets the correct answer (examples A, B, and E), but much of the time her answer is not the correct product.

If you were Marsha's teacher, what corrective procedures might you follow? Describe two instructional activities which you think would help Marsha multiply decimals correctly.

1._____

_____

_____

2._____

_____

_____

When your responses are complete, turn to page 118 and see if your suggestions are among the alternatives described.

Error Pattern D–D–1

from Ted's paper on page 51.

If you found Ted's error pattern, your results are the same as the erroneous computation shown below.

D.
$$\begin{array}{r} .852 \\ 3\overline{)2.57} \\ \underline{24} \\ 17 \\ \underline{15} \\ 2 \end{array}$$

E.
$$\begin{array}{r} 13.34 \\ .7\overline{)9.35} \\ \underline{7} \\ 23 \\ \underline{21} \\ 25 \\ \underline{21} \\ 4 \end{array}$$

Ted misses examples because of the way he handles remainders. If division does not "come out even" when taken as far as digits given in the dividend, Ted writes the remainder as an extension of the quotient. He may believe this is the same as writing R2 after the quotient for a division problem with whole numbers. Some children, having studied division with decimals, thereafter use a procedure similar to Ted's when dividing whole numbers. For example, 400 divided by 7 is computed as 57.1.

Ted needs help. How would you help him? Describe at least two instructional activities you believe would correct his error pattern.

1. _____

_____

_____

2. _____

_____

_____

After you have described at least two activities, turn to page 118 and compare your suggestions with the suggestions listed there.

Error Pattern S-M-1

from Margaret's paper on page 52.

Using Margaret's error pattern, examples D and E would be completed as they appear below.

D.
$$\begin{array}{r} \overset{5}{\cancel{6}} \text{ yards,} \overset{1}{\ } \text{1 foot} \\ - \ 2 \text{ yards, } 2 \text{ feet} \\ \hline 3 \text{ yards, } 9 \text{ feet} \end{array}$$

E.
$$\begin{array}{r} \overset{2}{\cancel{3}} \text{ quarts,} \overset{1}{\ } \text{1 cup} \\ - \ 1 \text{ quart, } 3 \text{ cups} \\ \hline 1 \text{ quart, } 8 \text{ cups} \end{array}$$

Margaret is regrouping in order to subtract just as she does when subtracting whole numbers expressed with base 10 numeration. She always crosses out the left figure and writes one less above it, then places a one in front of the right figure. This technique often produces a correct result when the relationship between the two measurement units is a base 10 relationship (see example B, page 52), but the results are incorrect whenever other relationships exist.

How would *you* help Margaret? Describe at least two instructional activities you believe would make it possible for Margaret to subtract correctly in measurement situations.

1. _____

_____

_____

2. _____

_____

_____

After you have written at least two descriptions, turn to page 120 and see if any of your activities are among the suggestions listed there.

4

Helping Children
Correct Error Patterns
in Computation

Whenever an error pattern is identified within a child's written work, corrective or remedial instruction needs to be provided so he will be able to replace his erroneous procedure with a useful algorithm. Only then can he make adequate use of computational procedures as tools. When a child solves mathematical problems and explores topics of interest, skill in computation permits him to expand his horizons conceptually.

In this chapter are descriptions of instructional activities which may be useful in helping children correct specific patterns of error. It is always important for the teacher to have in mind more than one instructional strategy; therefore, several activities are suggested for each error pattern. As you examine an error pattern, consider your own suggestions for providing remedial instruction. Do you find your suggestions among those recorded on the succeeding pages?

Selected materials that can be used in remedial instruction are described in Appendix E, and addresses are included so that you can write for further descriptive or purchasing information if you choose. Many of these materials are referred to in the pages which follow.

Error Pattern A-W-1

from pages 20 *and* 54.

What instructional activities did you suggest to help correct the error pattern illustrated? See if your suggestions are among those listed below.

E.
$$\begin{array}{r} 43 \\ + 65 \\ \hline 108 \end{array}$$

F.
$$\begin{array}{r} 88 \\ + 39 \\ \hline 1117 \end{array}$$

Note: Be sure to extend your diagnosis by interviewing the student. Let him "think out loud" for you. Unless you do this you will not even know if he is adding the ones or the tens first.

1. *Use bundles of ten and single sticks.* Show both addends, then "make a ten" as may have been done in past instruction. Emphasize that we always need to start with the single sticks. Apply a rule for exchanging or regrouping if it is possible. Then make ten bundles of ten, if possible, and apply the rule again. With paper and pencil, record what is done *step-by-step*.

2. *Show both addends on a computing abacus.* Proceed as above.

3. *Provide the student with a set of numerals (0–9) and a frame for the answer.* Each box of the frame should be of a size which will enclose only one digit. Let the student use the cardboard or plastic numerals to record sums for problems. This activity should help the student remember to apply the rule for exchanging.

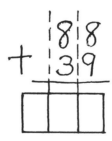

4. *Play chip-trading games.* To develop the idea for exchanging many for one, play games in which the values of chips are defined in terms of our numeration place-value pattern. However, it is easier to begin with bases less than ten. A child rolls a die and receives as many units as indicated on the die. He then exchanges for higher valued chips according to the rule of the game (five for one if base five, ten for one if base ten). Play proceeds similarly. The first child to get a specific chip of a high value wins. Such games are described in *Chip Trading Activities, Book I* (See Appendix E).

Error Pattern A-W-2

from pages 21 *and* 55.

What instructional activities do you suggest to help Mary correct the error pattern illustrated? See if your suggestions are among those described below.

E.
$$
\begin{array}{r}
254 \\
+535 \\
\hline 789
\end{array}
$$

F.
$$
\begin{array}{r}
\overset{3\ 2}{618} \\
+782 \\
\hline 1112
\end{array}
$$

1. *Approximate sums.* Even *before* computing, the sum can be estimated. For instance, in example **F** it can be determined in advance that the sum is more than 1300.

2. *Use a game board and a bank.* Help children understand place values and begin computation with units by making the algorithm a record of moves in a game. For example, base ten blocks can be used on a gameboard. To compute example **F**, the child would place 6 hundreds, 1 ten, and 8 unit blocks in the upper row. Then he sorts blocks for 782 in the second row. Beginning with the units (at the arrow), the child collects 10 units if he can (for this is a base 10 game) and moves all remaining units below the heavy line. If he has been able to collect 10 units, they are traded at the bank for 1 ten; the ten is then placed above the other tens in the shaded place. (At first many children want to verify the equivalence of what goes into the bank and what comes out by placing the 10 units in a row and matching them with 1 ten.) As the child continues, he collects 10 tens if he can, and

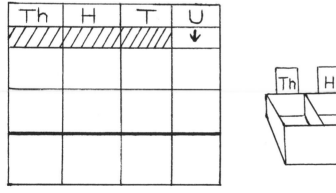

Game Board

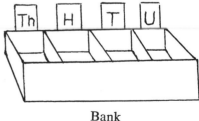

Bank

then moves all remaining tens below the heavy line. If he has been able to collect 10 tens, they are traded at the bank for 1 hundred, and the hundred is placed above the other hundreds in the shaded place. Finally, the child collects 10 hundreds if he can and moves all remaining hundreds below the heavy line. If he has been able to collect 10 hundreds they are traded at the bank for 1 thousand, and the thousand is placed in the shaded area at the top of the column for thousands. As it is not possible to collect 10 thousands, the one remaining thousand is brought

Th	H	T	U ↓
	□ □ □ □ □ □	〇	□ □□ □ □□□□
	□ □□ □□□	〇〇〇 〇〇〇	□ □

below the heavy line. As the child computes the sum on paper, he records the number of blocks in each region every time trading is completed. When the record is finished, the algorithm is completed.

Error Pattern A-W-3

from pages 22 and 56.

You have written suggestions for helping Carol, who was using the error pattern illustrated. Are your suggestions among those listed below?

F.
$$\begin{array}{r} 26 \\ + \ \ 3 \\ \hline 11 \end{array}$$

G.
$$\begin{array}{r} 60 \\ + 24 \\ \hline 84 \end{array}$$

H.
$$\begin{array}{r} 74 \\ + \ 5 \\ \hline 16 \end{array}$$

Note: An interview with the child may provide very helpful information. Is the child able to explain the examples which were worked correctly? Does the child identify tens and units and reason that units must be added to units and tens must be added to tens?

1. *Show each addend with base ten blocks.* After the child shows both addends, have him collect the units and record the total number of units. He can then collect the tens and record the total number of tens.

2. *Show addends with sticks or toothpicks.* Bundles of ten and single sticks (or toothpicks) can be used. Proceed as with base ten blocks.

3. *Draw a line to separate tens and units.* This procedure may help with the mechanics of notation if the child understands the need to add units to units and tens to tens.

$$\begin{array}{c|c} T & U \\ \hline & 3 \\ + 2 & 6 \\ \hline 2 & 9 \end{array} \qquad \begin{array}{c|c} T & U \\ \hline 6 & 0 \\ + 2 & 4 \\ \hline 8 & 4 \end{array} \qquad \begin{array}{c|c} T & U \\ \hline 7 & 4 \\ + & 5 \\ \hline 7 & 9 \end{array}$$

Error Pattern A-W-4

from pages 23 and 56.

You have suggested instructional activities for helping Dorothy or any child using this error pattern. Are your suggestions among those listed below?

$$\text{E.} \quad \begin{array}{r} {}^146 \\ + 8 \\ \hline 134 \end{array} \qquad \text{F.} \quad \begin{array}{r} {}^198 \\ + 3 \\ \hline 131 \end{array}$$

Note: The following suggestions assume that the child is *not* confusing these higher decade situations with multiplication.

1. *Explain the addition with ones and tens.* Have the child explain the addition to you in terms of ones (or units) and tens. If his understanding of place value is adequate, this procedure may be sufficient to clear up the problem. It may be necessary to have the child use base ten blocks, a place-value chart, or an abacus to work out the problem.

2. *Label tens and units.* Have the child label each column. The use of squared paper may also help if only one digit is written in each square.

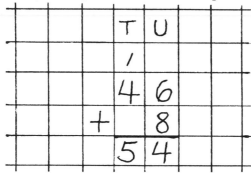

3. *Make higher decade sequences.* Help the child discover the pattern illustrated (at the top of page 88), then have him complete similar sequences. He may want to make up a few patterns all on his own.

$$
\begin{array}{r} 6 \\ +\ 8 \\ \hline 14 \end{array}
\quad
\begin{array}{r} 16 \\ +\ 8 \\ \hline 24 \end{array}
\quad
\begin{array}{r} 26 \\ +\ 8 \\ \hline 34 \end{array}
\quad
\begin{array}{r} 36 \\ +\ 8 \\ \hline 44 \end{array} \ldots
$$

Error Pattern S-W-1

from pages 24 and 57.

You have described instructional activities to help correct the error pattern illustrated below. Are your activities among those described?

E.
$$
\begin{array}{r} 458 \\ -\ 372 \\ \hline 126 \end{array}
$$

F.
$$
\begin{array}{r} 241 \\ -\ 96 \\ \hline 255 \end{array}
$$

Note: Be sure to extend your diagnosis by interviewing the child and letting him think out loud as he works similar examples. Does he use the erroneous procedure only with larger numbers? Does the child, on his own initiative, question the reasonableness of his answers? (In example F, the result is larger than the sum.)

1. *Use bundles of 100, bundles of ten and single sticks.*   Let the student show the "number altogether," the sum. Pose the problem of removing the number of sticks shown by the lower numeral. Trading or exchanging as needed could be done at a trading post or a bank. Any verbal problems presented in this context should describe "take-away" rather than comparison situations. Eventually, guidance should be provided to help the student remove ones first, then tens, etc.

2. *Use base ten blocks.*   Proceed as above.

3. *Use an abacus.*   Proceed as above. However, trading will not be for the same number of sticks or the same amount of wood. Trading will be based upon the more abstract notion of equal value.

4. *Use a place-value chart.*   Proceed similarly.

5. *Use real money.*   Only dollar bills, dimes, and pennies will be needed to show the amount indicated by the sum. Let the child set aside the amount indicated by the given addend, exchanging money as necessary at a bank. If this procedure is to point toward the computation, guidance should be given eventually to help the student set aside the pennies first, then dimes, and then dollars.

Error Pattern S-W-2

from pages 25 and 58.

You have described two instructional procedures for helping a child using this error pattern. Are the activities you suggested for George similar to any of the activities described below?

D.
$$\begin{array}{r} 2\overset{6}{\cancel{7}}\overset{1}{3} \\ -\ 38 \\ \hline 235 \end{array}$$

E.
$$\begin{array}{r} 2\overset{7}{\cancel{8}}\overset{1}{5} \\ -\ 63 \\ \hline 2112 \end{array}$$

Note: Helpful instruction will emphasize (1) the ability to distinguish between subtraction problems requiring regrouping in order to use basic subtraction facts and subtraction problems not requiring regrouping, and (2) mechanics of notation.

1. *Use a physical representation for the minuend (sum).* If the minuend of example E is represented physically (with base blocks or bundles of sticks), questions can be posed such as "Can I take away 3 units *without* trading?" "When do I need to trade and when is it not necessary for me to trade?"

2. *Replace computation with yes or no.* Focus on the critical skill of distinguishing by presenting a row of subtraction problems for which the differences are *not* to be computed. Have the child simply write yes or no for each example to indicate his decision whether regrouping is or is not needed. If this is difficult, physical materials should be available for the child to use. (See activity 1 above.)

3. *Use squared paper.* Have the student use squared paper for computation with the rule that only one digit can be written within each square. Before computing each example it may be helpful to review the place value of each column of squares.

4. *Estimate differences.* Before each problem is solved, have the student estimate the answer. Encourage statements like "more than 300" or "less than 500" rather than exact answers.

Error Pattern S-W-3

from pages 26 *and* 59.

You have described two instructional activities you think would help children like Donna with this zero difficulty. Are any of your suggestions among those listed below?

E.
$$446$$
$$-302$$
$$\overline{104}$$

F.
$$760$$
$$-230$$
$$\overline{530}$$

1. *Use sets and record number sentences.* In a demonstration with simple subtraction facts show the sum with a set of objects. Next, remove a subset of as many objects as the known addend. Finally, record the missing addend as the number of objects remaining. After demonstrating the process, let the child having difficulty remove a subset from a set of 9 objects or less while you record the number sentence as a record of what is done. Encourage the child to remove the empty set. Then reverse the process and you demonstrate while the child records with a number sentence. Include many examples of removing the empty set.

2. *Use base blocks or bundled sticks to picture the computation.* Show the sum of a given subtraction problem. Sit beside the child and arrange the materials so that units are to the right and hundreds to the left as in the algorithm. For example

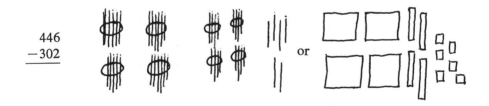

E, beginning with the units, remove the number (of sticks or blocks) shown by the given addend. After removing a subset of 2 units, record the fact that 4 units remain. After removing an empty set of tens, record the fact that 4 tens remain, etc. For another example, let the child remove the subsets while you record the number remaining. Finally, as you remove the subsets, have the child record the number remaining each time.

3. *Try a sorting game.* If the child has been introduced to the multiplication facts for zero, there may be confusion between the zero property for multiplication and

the zero properties for other operations. For the zero facts of arithmetic, cards can be prepared showing open number sentences similar to the ones shown. (Vertical

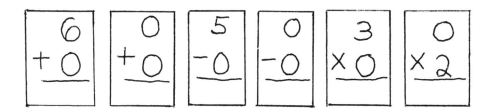

notation is suggested in this case because it appears in the algorithm.) It may be appropriate to include division number sentences as well, *e.g.*, $0 \div 3 = ?$ As an individual activity or as a game for two, the cards can be sorted into two sets—those with zero for the answer and those which do not have zero for an answer.

Error Pattern S-W-4

from pages 27 *and* 60.

Do you find, among the suggestions listed below, your suggestions for helping Barbara, who has the difficulty illustrated?

E.
$$
\begin{array}{r}
\overset{3}{\cancel{4}}\overset{1}{3}6 \\
-\ 172 \\
\hline
264
\end{array}
$$

F.
$$
\begin{array}{r}
\overset{4}{\cancel{6}}\overset{1}{2}\overset{1}{5} \\
-\ 348 \\
\hline
187
\end{array}
$$

Note: Asking a child to check his computation may accomplish little in this situation. "Adding up" may only confirm that individual subtraction facts have been correctly completed. (In example F, $7 + 8 = 15$, $8 + 4 = 12$, and $1 + 3 = 4$.) The following activities are suggested to help the child keep in mind the *total quantity* from which a lesser number is being subtracted.

1. *Use base ten blocks to show the sum (minuend).* Pointing to the subtrahend, ask, "What trading must we do so we can take away this many?" As appropriate, trade a ten for ones and *immediately* record the action; then trade a hundred for tens and record that action. Stress the need to proceed step by step. Have the child trade and remove blocks while you record the action, then reverse the process. While you trade and remove blocks, let the child make the record.

2. *Use a place-value chart.* Proceed in a manner similar to that suggested for base ten blocks.

3. *Use bundles of 100, bundles of ten and single sticks.* Proceed as above.

4. *Use an abacus.* Again, proceed as above.

5. *Use real money.* Have the child show the sum, then ask him to set aside the amount indicated by the given addend, trading at a bank as necessary. Again, the record should be made step-by-step.

6. *Use expanded notation.* Have the child rename the sum to a name which makes possible the use of basic subtraction facts. In this example, $600 + 20 + 5$ was renamed as $600 + 10 + 15$, then $600 + 10 + 15$ was renamed as $\overline{500 + 110} + 15$. Base ten blocks can be used to verify such equivalences.

$$
\begin{array}{rcl}
625 & = & \overset{500}{\cancel{600}} + \overset{\overset{110}{\cancel{20}}}{\cancel{20}} + \overset{15}{\cancel{5}} \\
-\ 348 & = & 300 + 40 + 8 \\
\hline
& & 200 + 70 + 7 = 277
\end{array}
$$

Error Pattern S-W-5

from pages 28 *and* 61.

Are your suggestions for helping Sam among the suggestions listed below? He has the illustrated difficulties.

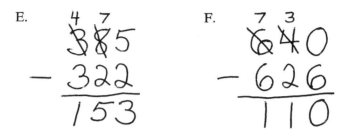

Note: Suggestions 3 and 4 are primarily for dealing with the zero difficulty illustrated in this error pattern.

1. *Use base blocks or bundled sticks to picture the sum (minuend).* Specific procedures are outlined with Error Pattern S-W-4.

2. *Estimate before computing.* Have the child estimate his answer. A number line showing at least hundreds and tens may be helpful for this purpose. Ask, "Will the answer be more than a hundred? . . . less than a hundred?"

3. *Use a learning center for renaming.* For Sam and others with similar difficulties, a simple learning center could be set up to help them rename a minuend and select the most useful name for that number in a specific subtraction problem. One possibility is to have a sorting task in which the child decides which cards show another name for a given number and which show an entirely different number. A second task would be to consider all the different names for the given number and decide which of the names would be most useful for computing subtraction problems having the given number for the minuend. Ask, "Which name will let us use the subtraction facts we know?"

4. *Use a game board and a bank.*   Make the subtraction algorithm a record of moves in a game. Use the game board and bank pictured with Error Pattern A-W-2 but have the child picture *only the minuend* with base blocks or similar materials. The subtrahend should be shown with numeral cards to indicate how much wood is to be removed from the minuend set of wood. Begin with units and trade one ten for ten units if necessary; then place the units card and as many unit pieces of wood aside. The units that remain should be brought below the heavy line. For the tens, repeat by trading one hundred for ten tens if needed in order to have enough tens pieces to go with the numeral card below. Set aside the numeral card and the indicated number of tens; then bring the remaining tens below the line and continue the procedure. Make a step-by-step record of the child's moves in the game by recording each move with the written algorithm. Later, let the child record your moves or those of another child.

Th	H	T	U
////	////	////	↓
	□ □	/ / / /	▫ ▫ ▫
	1	8	5

Game Board Used for Subtraction

Error Pattern M-W-1

from pages 29 *and* 62.

How would you help a student such as Bob correct the error pattern illustrated? Are the activities you described similar to any of those below?

D.
$$
\begin{array}{r}
\overset{4}{9}8 \\
\times\ 56 \\
\hline
588 \\
490 \\
\hline
5488
\end{array}
$$

E.
$$
\begin{array}{r}
\overset{3}{8}6 \\
\times\ 45 \\
\hline
430 \\
354 \\
\hline
3970
\end{array}
$$

Note: The following activities emphasize place value, the distributive property, and proper mechanics of notation.

1. *Use more partial products and no crutch.* The following algorithm can be related to an array which is partitioned twice. When the student is able to use this

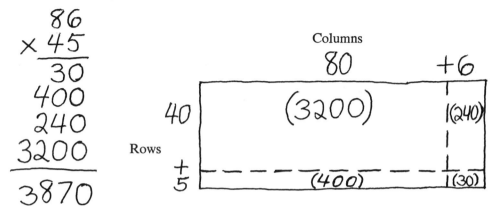

algorithm with ease, let him try to combine the first two partial products (and also the last two) by *remembering* the number of tens and the number of hundreds. Do not encourage the use of a crutch in this situation.

2. *Make two problems.* When the student is able to compute the product in this way, encourage him to try remembering his crutch "because such crutches are sometimes confusing in multiplication and division problems." When he can compute easily without recording the crutch, convert to a more standard algorithm by placing the same partial products *under* the example.

3. *Record tens within partial products.* Instead of writing "crutch" numerals above the example, use lightly written, half-sized numerals within each of the partial products to record the number of tens to be remembered.

4. *Apply the commutative and associative principles.* This technique should be especially helpful if the student has difficulty in processing open number sentences like $5 \times 80 = ?$; $40 \times 6 = ?$; and $40 \times 80 = ?$ These number sentences are parts of example E and suggest a prerequisite skill for such examples; namely, application of the commutative and associative principles where one of the factors is a multiple of a power of ten. The error pattern may result, in part, from thinking of all digits as ones and the inability to think of tens, hundreds, etc., when using basic multiplication facts. After the associative principle is introduced with one-digit factors (perhaps with the aid of a three-dimensional arrangement of cubic units) let the student think through examples such as:

$$40 \times 6 = (4 \times 10) \times 6$$
$$= (10 \times 4) \times 6$$
$$= 10 \times (4 \times 6)$$
$$= 10 \times 24$$
$$= 240$$

When the student generalizes this procedure, he will be able to compute the product of a one-digit number and a multiple of a power of ten *in one step.*

Cautions

In general, written crutches are to be encouraged if they are useful and help the child understand what he is doing. However, they can be confusing when multiplying by a two-digit multiplier. Problems such as $5 \times 86 = ?$ occur within division algorithms where use of a written crutch is impractical. For these reasons students should be encouraged to remember such crutches.

There is a very real danger in proceeding to a standard algorithm too quickly. A new, more efficient procedure is best introduced as a shortcut of an already understood algorithm. Zeros help a student think in terms of place value. Do not insist that the units zero in the second and succeeding partial products be dropped. (Pencil lead is not that expensive!)

Error Pattern M-W-2

from pages 30 *and* 62.

In the error pattern illustrated below, the child forgets to add the number of tens recorded as a crutch. Which of the instructional activities you suggested as help for this child are similar to activities described below?

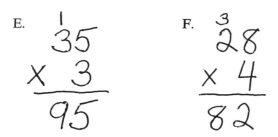

1. *Use partial products.* Introduce the following algorithm, possibly as a record of multiplying with parts of a partitioned array. If the child has previously used this algorithm and he uses it successfully, it may still be wise to return to the longer

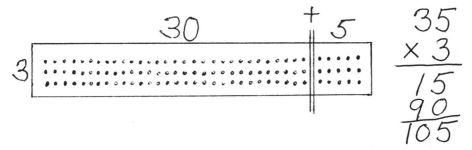

procedure so that instruction can proceed from a position of strength. Before returning to the standard algorithm, it may be helpful to have the child encircle the numeral to be remembered.

2. *Record a reminder below the bar.* Instead of a small numeral written above the multiplicand, introduce the idea that a reminder can be recorded as follows:

$$\begin{array}{r} 28 \\ \times\ 4 \\ \hline {}^{3}\ \ 2 \end{array} \qquad \begin{array}{r} 28 \\ \times\ 4 \\ \hline 1\overset{3}{1}2 \end{array}$$

Step a   Step b

This procedure is a convenient bridge between the algorithm using partial products and the standard algorithm.

$$\begin{array}{r} 27 \\ \times\ 3 \\ \hline 21 \\ 60 \\ \hline 81 \end{array} \longrightarrow \begin{array}{r} 2\!\!\!/7 \\ \times\ 3 \\ \hline 8\!\!\!/1 \end{array} \longrightarrow \begin{array}{r} 2\!\!\!/7 \\ \times\ 3 \\ \hline 8\ 1 \end{array}$$

Error Pattern M-W-3

from pages 31 *and* 63.

You have described two instructional activities for helping Joe and other students who have adopted the error pattern illustrated. Are your suggestions included in the activities described below?

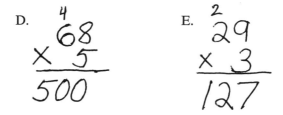

D.
$$\overset{4}{68} \times 5 \over 500$$

E.
$$\overset{2}{29} \times 3 \over 127$$

1. *Use partial products.* Such an algorithm is easily developed as a step-by-step record of what is done when an array is partitioned. Help the child determine the

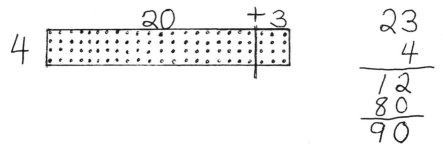

order in which the multiplication and addition occur; lead him to generalize and state the sequence. In the example above, the 2 tens are multiplied by the 4; later the 1 ten is added to the 8 tens.

2. *Write the crutch below the bar.* Instead of the child writing a reminder in the conventional way, have him make a small numeral below the bar to remind him to add *just before* recording a product.

3. *Practice examples of the form* $(a \times b) + c$. Sometimes a child appears to understand the algorithm and can verbalize the proper procedure correctly, but while using the algorithm he adopts careless procedures. Such a child may be helped by having him practice examples such as $(4 \times 2) + 1 = ?$ and $(3 \times 6) + 2 = ?$, thereby reinforcing the proper sequence. The child should be helped to relate this kind of practice to his difficulty in the multiplication algorithm.

Error Pattern M-W-4

from pages 32 *and* 64.

Are either of the instructional activities you suggested among those listed below?

$$
\begin{array}{r}
\text{E.} \quad 621 \\
\times \ 23 \\
\hline
1243
\end{array}
\qquad
\begin{array}{r}
\text{F.} \quad \overset{2}{5}17 \\
463 \\
\hline
2081
\end{array}
$$

1. *Use the distributive property.* Have the child rewrite each problem as two problems. Later relate each partial product to the partial products in the conventional algorithm.

$$
\begin{array}{r}
621 \\
\times \ 23 \\
\end{array}
\longrightarrow
\begin{array}{r}
621 \\
\times \ 20 \\
\hline
?
\end{array}
+
\begin{array}{r}
621 \\
\times \ 3 \\
\hline
?
\end{array}
$$

If the child does not understand why the sum of the two multiplication problems is the same number as the product in the original problem, partition an array and label the parts.

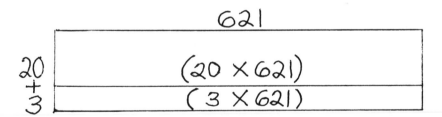

2. *Use a paper mask.* Cover the multiplier so only one digit will show at a time. After multiplication by the units digit is completed, the mask can be moved to the left so that only the tens digit is visible. Later, the hundreds digit can be highlighted. With each digit, emphasize the need to do a complete multiplication problem. Also stress proper placement of each partial product.

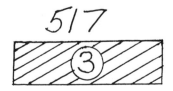

Error Pattern D-W-1

from pages 33 *and* 65.

How might you help Jim correct the erroneous procedure in the illustration? Are the instructional activities you described similar to any of the activities listed below?

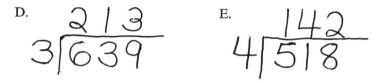

D. $3\overline{\smash{\big)}639} = 213$ E. $4\overline{\smash{\big)}518} = 142$

Note: To help the student who has adopted such an error pattern, activities need to emphasize place value in the dividend and the total quantity of the dividend. Procedures which can be understood in relation to concrete referents are needed instead of an assortment of rules to be applied in a mechanical way. In essence, a reintroduction to a division algorithm is needed.

1. *Use number rods to redevelop the algorithm.* Teach the child a computational procedure as a step-by-step record of activity with objects. For the problem $54 \div 3 = ?$, the child can show the dividend as 5 ten-rods and 4 unit-rods using base blocks, Cuisenaire rods, Stern blocks, or even single sticks and bundles of sticks. Interpret the divisor as the number of equivalent sets to be formed. For example, in $54 \div 3 = ?$, objects are to be distributed among three sets.

To begin, 1 ten-rod is placed in each of the three sets. Then a record is made to show this has been done. The record should also show that a total of 3 ten-rods have been removed from the dividend set (Step a). As the 2 remaining ten-rods cannot be distributed among three sets, they are traded for 20 units and joined with the other 4 unit-rods. This procedure is shown by "bringing down" the 4 (Step b). The 24 unit-rods are then distributed equally among the three sets and the record is completed (Step c).

Step a	Step b	Step c

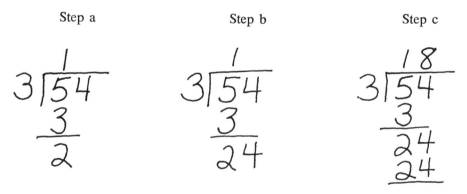

2. *Estimate quotient figures.* Use open number sentences such as $3 \times ? \leq 65$ with the rule that the number to be found is the largest multiple of a power of 10

which will make the number sentence true. To record the resulting partial quotients, one of the following algorithms would be especially useful:

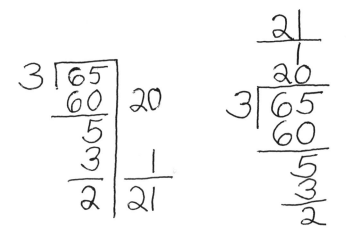

3. *Focus on skill in multiplying multiples of powers of ten by a single digit.* This skill, used in the above activities, may need to be developed independently of a division algorithm. Patterns can be observed from such data as the following display.

$$2 \times 3 = 6 \qquad\qquad 2 \times 3 = 6$$
$$2 \times 30 = 60 \qquad\qquad 20 \times 3 = 60$$
$$2 \times 300 = 600 \qquad 200 \times 3 = 600$$

It is possible to present a more detailed explanation related to a $2 \times 3 \times 10$ rectangular prism of unit cubes or to an application of mathematical principles.

$$2 \times 30 = 2 \times (3 \times 10)$$
$$= (2 \times 3) \times 10$$
$$= 6 \times 10$$
$$= 60$$

Error Pattern D-W-2

from pages 34 *and* 66.

Below are illustrations of Gail's error pattern in division of whole numbers. Are the instructional activities you suggested to help this child among those described?

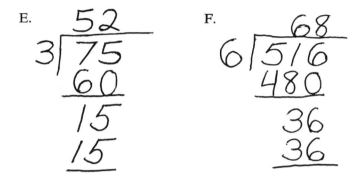

1. *Emphasize place value in estimating quotient figures.*   Have the child use open number sentences such as $3 \times ? \leq 70$ and $3 \times ? \leq 15$ while thinking through example E. Number sentences should be completed using the following rule: When dividing 7 tens, the missing number is the largest multiple of ten which will make the number sentence true. For $3 \times ? \leq 70$, $? = 20$. Similarly, when dividing 15 ones the missing number is the largest multiple of one which will make the number sentence true. For larger numbers, similar rules apply.

2. *Use a different algorithm.*   At least temporarily, choose an algorithm that will show the value of each partial quotient. In each of the algorithms shown, the 8 in the

quotient of example F is shown as 80, thereby emphasizing proper placement of quotient figures. After the student is able to use such algorithms, a transition to the standard computational procedure can be made, if desired, by recording quotients differently. In example F, the first quotient figure would be recorded as 8 in the tens place instead of as 80.

3. *Develop skill in multiplying multiples of powers of 10.*   This skill is necessary for rational use of any of the division algorithms illustrated. Exercises can be written to facilitate observation of patterns by the student.

$$6 \times 4 = 24$$
$$6 \times 40 = 240$$
$$6 \times 400 = 2400$$

Or, a more detailed explanation can be developed.

$$6 \times 400 = 6 \times (4 \times 100)$$
$$= (6 \times 4) \times 100$$
$$= 24 \times 100$$
$$= 2400$$

4. *Estimate the quotient before computing.* Frequently, quotients resulting from the erroneous algorithm are quite unreasonable. If intelligent estimating is followed by computing, and the estimate and the quotient are then compared, the student may rethink his computational procedure.

Error Pattern D-W-3

from pages 35 and 67.

You have suggested activities for helping John, who was using the error pattern illustrated. Are your suggestions among those listed below?

E.

$$
\begin{array}{r}
32 r 3 \\
9 \overline{)2721} \\
27 \\
\hline
21 \\
18 \\
\hline
3
\end{array}
$$

F.

$$
\begin{array}{r}
78 r 2 \\
6 \overline{)4250} \\
42 \\
\hline
50 \\
48 \\
\hline
2
\end{array}
$$

1. *Use lined paper turned 90°.*   It may be that having the child use vertically lined paper (or manila cross-sectioned paper) will clear up the problem. The omission of one digit becomes very obvious when such forms are used for practice.

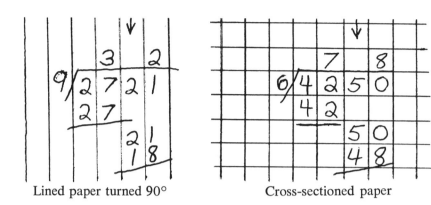

Lined paper turned 90°   Cross-sectioned paper

2. *Use the pyramid algorithm.*   At least temporarily, use an algorithm that emphasizes place value. If the pyramid algorithm has been learned by the child earlier in the instructional program, ask him to solve some of the troublesome examples using it in order to see if he can figure out why he is having difficulty now. If the pyramid algorithm is new to the child, he may enjoy trying a new procedure which is a bit easier to understand.

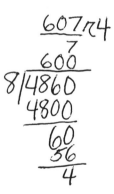

3. *Estimate the quotient before beginning computation.*   The practice of recording an estimated quotient before computing may be sufficient to overcome the problem, especially if the error is not present in every such example and careless writing of quotient figures is a major cause of the difficulty.

Error Pattern D-W-4

  from pages 36 and 68.

Are your suggestions for helping a child like Anita with the error pattern shown below among those suggestions listed?

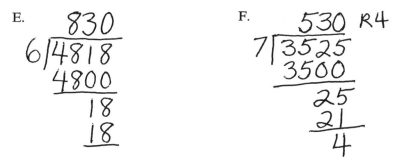

E.
$$\begin{array}{r} 830 \\ 6\overline{)4818} \\ 4800 \\ \hline 18 \\ 18 \end{array}$$

F.
$$\begin{array}{r} 530 \ \text{R4} \\ 7\overline{)3525} \\ 3500 \\ \hline 25 \\ 21 \\ \hline 4 \end{array}$$

1. *Develop skill in multiplying multiples of powers of ten by a single-digit number.* Patterns such as this one can be observed. As the pattern is generalized and skill in

$$3 \times 6 = 18 \qquad\qquad 7 \times 3 = 21$$
$$30 \times 6 = 180 \qquad\quad 7 \times 30 = 210$$
$$300 \times 6 = 1800 \quad 7 \times 300 = 2100$$

such multiplication is developed, help the child see specific points within the division algorithm where this skill is applied.

2. *Use the pyramid algorithm.* Using an algorithm with partial quotients may adequately demonstrate the need for a zero in the tens place of the quotient.

$$\begin{array}{r} 803 \\ 3 \\ 800 \\ 6\overline{)4818} \\ 4800 \\ \hline 18 \\ 18 \end{array}$$

3. *Use base 10 blocks.* In the example 4818 ÷ 6 = ?, have the child show 4818 with 4 thousand-blocks, 8 hundred-blocks, 1 ten-block, and 8 unit-blocks. Write the problem, and interpret the problem as partitioning the blocks into 6 sets of equal number. As it is not possible to parcel out 4 thousand-blocks among 6 sets, it is necessary to exchange the 4 thousand-blocks for an equal amount of wood, *i.e.,* for 40 hundred-blocks. The 48 hundred-blocks are then parcelled out evenly among 6 sets. The 8 in the hundreds place is recorded to show that 8 hundred-blocks have been placed in each of the 6 sets, and the 4800 is written in the algorithm to show how many blocks have been taken from the initial pile of blocks. (The initial pile of blocks can be called the dividend pile.) After subtracting to see how many blocks remain in the initial pile, the resulting 18 should be compared with the 1 ten-block and 8 unit-blocks remaining to verify that the record (the algorithm) accurately describes what remains.

The next task is to parcel out ten-blocks among the 6 sets; however, the 1 ten-block cannot be partitioned among 6 sets. It is therefore necessary to exchange the 1 ten-block for an equal number—for 10 unit-blocks. Before exchanging, *have the child record in the algorithm with a zero that no ten-blocks are being partitioned* among the 6 sets. Finally, proceed to partition the 18 unit-blocks and complete the algorithm.

Error Pattern E-F-1

from pages 37 *and* 69

When attempting to change a fraction to lower terms, Greg used his own cancellation procedure. Which of the instructional activities you suggested as help for this child are similar to activities described below?

E. $\dfrac{16}{64} = \dfrac{1}{4}$ F. $\dfrac{14}{42} = \dfrac{1}{2}$

Note: You will probably want to extend your diagnosis to see if the child can interpret a fraction with some form of physical representation. If not, instruction should focus first of all upon the meaning or meanings of a fraction. The activities which follow are suggested with the assumption that the student has a basic understanding of the fraction idea.

1. *Emphasize prime factorizations.* Show that both the numerator and the denominator can be renamed as products. If the unique name for a number we call the prime factorization is used, common factors can be noted and the greatest common factor can be determined easily. When the fraction is rewritten with prime factorizations, the child's cancellation procedure *is* appropriate. If the student needs experience with prime numbers, play a game like Prime Drag (see Appendix E).

2. *Use the multiplicative identity to "go both ways."* Have the child use names for one of the form n/n when multiplying to rename a common fraction to higher terms. Then explore the question, How can we change the fraction back to the way it was? Show that both numerator and denominator can be divided by the same number without changing the value of the fraction.

3. *Interpret a fraction as a ratio of disjoint sets.* Construct disjoint sets to show both numerator and denominator and compare them. For the unit fraction $\frac{1}{4}$ and any fraction which is equivalent to $\frac{1}{4}$, the denominator is four times as great as the numerator. Have the child evaluate his written work keeping this relationship in mind.

Error Pattern E-F-2

from pages 38 *and* 69.

The error pattern illustrated was explained: "3 goes to 1, and 4 goes to 2." Are the instructional activities you suggested similar to any of the activities described below?

E. $$\frac{3}{4} = \frac{1}{2}$$ F. $$\frac{2}{8} = \frac{1}{4}$$

Note: It may be wise to extend the diagnosis to determine if the student is able to interpret a fraction as parts of a region or a set. If the student cannot, instruction should begin with a concept of a fraction. The following activities assume the student has such a basic understanding of a fraction even though a mechanical rule for changing a fraction to simplest terms was adopted.

1. *Use fractional parts of regions.*   Begin with reference to the unit, then show the given number with fractional parts. Do *not* restrict the instruction to pie shapes, but use rectangular shapes as well. Pose the question, "Can we use larger parts to

$$\frac{4}{6}$$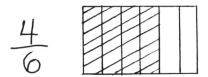

cover what we have exactly?" Record several "experiments" and note which are already in simplest terms. Then look for a mathematical rule for changing, *i.e.,* dividing both numerator and denominator by the same number.

2. *Look for a pattern in a list.*   Present a list of *correct* examples similar to the following ones. Have the student look for a pattern (a mathematical rule) for

$$\frac{6}{8} = \frac{3}{4}$$

$$\frac{4}{6} = \frac{2}{3}$$

changing. Test out the suggested pattern on other examples. When a correct procedure is found, use it to help determine which fractions can be changed to simpler terms and which are already in simplest terms.

3. *Make sets of equivalent fractions.*   Children can do this by successively subdividing regions. Record the resulting sets of equivalent fractions, with the smallest

$$\left\{ \frac{2}{3}, \frac{4}{6}, \frac{6}{9}, \frac{8}{12}, \circ \circ \circ \right\}$$

whole numbers first and larger numbers in order; then use the sets for finding simplest terms. Look for a relationship between any one fraction and the first fraction in the set.

4. *Have a race.* Play a board game in which players race their pieces forward along a track made up of sections, each of which is partitioned into twelfths. Players roll special dice, draw cards with fraction numerals, or draw unit regions for fractions. Possible fractions include $1/2$, $2/3$, $5/6$, $3/4$, and so forth. Moves forward are for the equivalent number of twelfths. An example of this kind of game can be found in the Introductory Cards of the Fraction Bars program (see Appendix E).

Error Pattern E-F-3

from pages 39 *and* 70.

In order to change to lowest terms, Sue divided the larger number by the smaller to determine the new numerator, and copied the larger number as the new denominator. Which of the remedial instructional activities you suggested are among the activities described below?

G. $\frac{3}{6} = \frac{2}{6}$ H. $\frac{6}{4} = \frac{1}{6}$

Note: There is some evidence that this child is only manipulating symbols in a mechanistic way and not even interpreting fractions as parts of unit regions. For example, the child's statement that $3/6 = 2/6$ suggests that an understanding of $3/6$ or $2/6$ as parts of a unit just is not present, or, if it is, it is a behavior associated with something like fraction pies, and it is not applied in other contexts. It may be wise to interview the child to determine how the child conceptualizes fractions before planning any remedial instruction.

1. *Match numerals with physical or diagrammatic representations.* To encourage the interpretation of a fraction in terms of real world referents, help the child learn and reinforce two behaviors:
   (a) When the child is given a physical or diagrammatic representation for a fraction, he writes the fraction or picks out a numeral card showing "how much." In an activity of this sort, be sure the child understands the given frame of reference, *i.e.,* the unit.
   (b) When the child is given a fractional numeral, he makes a representation for the fraction with blocks, parts of a unit region, sets, etc.; or he draws an appropriate diagrammatic representation.

2. *Order fraction cards.* Give the child a set of cards, each with a different fraction having the same denominator. Have him sequence the cards, thereby focusing on the fact that $3/6 \neq 2/6$. (It may be necessary to emphasize that the equality sign means "is the same as.") Encourage the child to refer to physical or diagrammatic representations as necessary to verify his decisions.

3. *Play "Can you make a whole?"* The child needs to recognize fractions which can be changed to a mixed number. Give the child a set of cards with a fraction on each card. Some of the cards should have proper or common fractions; others

should have improper fractions. The child plays the game by sorting the cards into two piles: those which will "make a whole" (those equal to or greater than 1) and those which will not "make a whole." A playing partner or teacher then picks two of the sorted cards to challenge, and the child uses physical representations to prove that the challenged fractions are sorted correctly. If two children are playing, they should take turns assuming sorting and challenging roles. More specific game rules and scoring procedures (if any) can be agreed upon by the children involved.

Additional suggestions for remedial activities are listed for pattern E-F-2 on pages 106 and 107. They are apt to be appropriate if the child is able to do the activities listed above.

Error Pattern A-F-1

from pages 40 *and* 71.

What instructional activities do you suggest to help Robbie correct the error pattern illustrated? See if your suggestions are among those illustrated below.

E. $\dfrac{3}{4} + \dfrac{1}{5} = \dfrac{4}{9}$ F. $\dfrac{2}{3} + \dfrac{5}{6} = \dfrac{7}{9}$

Note: You should extend your diagnosis by having the child complete a variety of tasks which assess subordinate skills for adding unlike fractions. Appendix D is a hierarchy of such tasks. If you prepare a diagnostic instrument with the hierarchy as a guide, order your examples from simple to complex. You may want to put them on cards or in a learning center. Because the error pattern is so similar to the multiplication algorithm, this may be a child who tends to carry over one situation into his perception of another. If so, avoid extensive practice at a given time on any single procedure.

1. *Replace computation with "horizontal" and "vertical."* When adding *un*like fractions, it is usually best to write the example vertically so the renaming can be recorded more easily. Have the child practice deciding which of several examples should be written vertically to facilitate computation and which can be computed horizontally.

2. *Use unit regions and parts of unit regions.* Have the child first represent each addend as fractional parts of a unit region. It will be necessary for the child to exchange some of the fractional parts so they are all of the same size (same denominator). The fractional parts can then be used to determine the total number of units. This procedure should be related step-by-step to the mechanics of notation in a written algorithm, probably an example written vertically so the renaming can be noted more easily.

3. *Estimate answers before computing.* This may require some practice locating fractions on a number line and ordering fractions written on cards. Use phrases like

"almost a half" and "a little less than one" when discussing problems. In example F, more than a half is added to a little less than one. The result should be about one and a half.

Error Pattern A-F-2

from pages 41 and 72.

How would you help a student such as Dave who uses the error pattern illustrated below? Are your suggestions included among the activities described?

D.
$$9\tfrac{1}{3} = \tfrac{3}{9}$$
$$+ \ 5\tfrac{5}{9} = \tfrac{5}{9}$$
$$\tfrac{8}{9}$$

E.
$$16\tfrac{3}{4} = \tfrac{3}{4}$$
$$+ \ 23\tfrac{1}{2} = \tfrac{2}{4}$$
$$\tfrac{5}{4} = 1\tfrac{1}{4}$$

1. *Estimate answers before computing.* Have the child record an estimated answer before he computes. Attention is thereby focused upon addition of the whole numbers. In example E, the child could note that a number greater than 16 added to a number greater than 23 will be a number greater than 39. Similarly, a number less than 17 added to a number less than 24 will be a number less than 41. The sum must be between 39 and 41.

2. *Emphasize the meaning of "equals."* Tell (or remind) the child that the equality sign means "is the same as." Have the child point to each equality sign in his work and explain why the numerals on either side of the sign are both names for the same number.

3. *Use unit regions and parts of unit regions.* This procedure should not be necessary for most students using the error pattern under consideration, but it can help some students become much more conscious of the whole numbers involved. If this procedure is to be followed, have the child first represent each addend with physical aids, *e.g.,* as a number of unit regions and as fractional parts of a region. It may then be necessary for the child to exchange some of the fractional parts so they are all of the same size (same denominator). The fractional parts can then be joined together and the unit regions can also be joined. Whenever it is possible, another unit region should be formed from the collection of fractional parts. This procedure should be related step-by-step to the mechanics of notation in the written algorithm.

Error Pattern A-F-3

from pages 42 and 73.

You have described at least two instructional activities you think would help Allen or any child with the difficulty illustrated. Are any of your suggestions among those listed below?

D.
$$\frac{1}{4} + \frac{1}{5} = \frac{5}{9} + \frac{4}{9} = \frac{9}{9}$$

E.
$$\frac{2}{5} + \frac{1}{2} = \frac{2}{7} + \frac{10}{7} = \frac{12}{7}$$

Note: Doctoring up an erroneous mechanical procedure by trying to substitute other purely mechanical procedures frequently results in a further confusion of arbitrary and meaningless procedures. Remediation should help the student use procedures which make sense to him.

1. *Find the l.c.m. (lowest common multiple) of two whole numbers.*   To help the child find the least common denominator for two fractions, work separately with the denominators as whole numbers. First make sure the child can generate sets of multiples for each whole number. If the student is able to identify the intersection set of two given sets, he will be able to find a set of *common* multiples. Finally, he can note which common multiple is *least* in value. This least common multiple is the most useful common denominator for adding the two fractions. To reinforce this skill, give the student examples where he only finds the least common denominator.

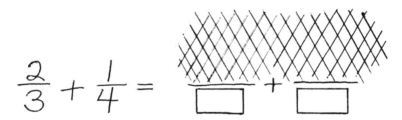

$$\frac{2}{3} + \frac{1}{4} =$$

2. *Use the property of one for multiplication and the idea of many names for a number.*   When the student can determine the least common denominator he will probably need specific help in changing one fraction to an equivalent fraction with a specified denominator. This is a specific skill which can be developed apart from the larger example.

$$\frac{2}{3} = \frac{\Box}{12}$$

If the child knows or can be taught how to multiply simple fractions, the property of one can be applied in renaming. The question posed is *"Which* name for one is useful?"

The useful name
for one

$$\frac{2}{3} \times 1 = \frac{\Box}{12} \qquad \frac{2}{3} \times \frac{\triangle}{\triangle} = \frac{\Box}{12} \qquad \frac{2}{3} \times \frac{4}{4} = \frac{\Box}{12}$$

Clue: $3 \times \triangle = 12$

3. *Change to a vertical algorithm.* A vertical algorithm permits the student to write simple equivalence statements for each renaming of a fraction.

$$+ \quad \begin{array}{l} \frac{2}{3} = \frac{2}{3} \times \frac{4}{4} = \frac{8}{12} \\ \frac{1}{4} = \frac{1}{4} \times \frac{3}{3} = \frac{3}{12} \\ \hline \frac{11}{12} \end{array}$$

Error Pattern S-F-1

from pages 43 *and* 74.

Are your suggestions for helping Andrew with the difficulty illustrated below among the suggestions listed?

E.
$$\begin{array}{r} 5\frac{1}{5} \\ - 3\frac{3}{5} \\ \hline 2\frac{2}{5} \end{array}$$

F.
$$\begin{array}{r} 1 \\ - \frac{1}{3} \\ \hline 1\frac{1}{3} \end{array}$$

Note: You will want to interview the child and have him think out loud as he works similar examples. Does the child question the reasonableness of his answers? In example F, the result is larger than the sum (minuend).

1. *Use fractional parts of a unit region.* Interpret the example as "take-away" subtraction and use fractional parts to show *only* the sum. If the child subtracts the whole numbers first, demonstrate that this procedure does not work; not enough remains so the fraction can be subtracted. Conclude that the fraction must be

subtracted first. Have the child exchange one of the units for an equivalent set of fractional parts in order to take away the quantity indicated by the subtrahend.

2. *Use crutches to facilitate renaming.* Record the exchange of fractional parts (suggested above) as a renaming of the sum. The sum is renamed so the fraction can be subtracted easily.

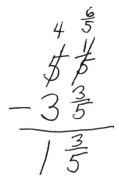

3. *Practice specific prerequisite skills.* Without computing, the child can decide which examples require renaming and which do not. The skill of renaming a mixed number in order to subtract can also be practiced. You will get ideas for other prerequisite skills from Appendix D, for most, if not all, of the tasks in the addition hierarchy found there apply equally to subtraction.

$$2\frac{1}{3} = 1\frac{4}{3} \qquad\qquad 3\frac{1}{2} = 2\frac{3}{2}$$

Error Pattern S-F-2

from pages 44 *and* 75.

You have described activities for helping Don, who is using the error pattern illustrated. Are your suggestions among those listed below?

D.
$$6\frac{5}{8} = 6\frac{5}{8}$$
$$-\;3\frac{1}{4} = 3\frac{2}{8}$$
$$\overline{\qquad 3\frac{3}{8}}$$

E.
$$4\frac{3}{8} = 4\overset{3}{\cancel{8}}\overset{\cancel{8}}{}$$
$$-1\frac{1}{2} = 1\frac{4}{8}$$
$$\overline{\qquad 2\frac{4}{8} = 2\frac{1}{2}}$$

1. *Use fractional parts of a region.* The child can rename mixed numbers by exchanging a unit region for fractional parts. For example, in problem E, he can exchange 1 of the unit regions for 8 eighths and place them with the 3 other eighths. He should record his findings by writing 4⅜ = 3¹¹⁄₈.

2. *Find many names for a mixed number.* Have the child make several names for a given number. For example, $4\% = 3^{1}\% = 2^{1}\% = 1^{2}\%$. For each unit subtracted it is necessary to add $\%$ in order to keep the same numerical value for the mixed number. Guide the child in applying this skill in subtraction by asking the questions: "Do I need to rename? What name will be most useful?"

Error Pattern S-F-3

from pages 45 and 76.

Do you find among the suggestions listed below your suggestions for helping Chuck who has the difficulty illustrated?

E. $6\frac{2}{3} - 3\frac{1}{6} = 3\frac{1}{3}$ F. $4\frac{5}{8} - 1\frac{3}{4} = 3\frac{2}{4}$

Note: Extended diagnosis is probably wise. Most if not all of the subordinate skills suggested in the addition hierarchy found in Appendix D apply equally to subtraction.

1. *Replace computation with "horizontal" and "vertical."* When subtracting with unlike fractions and with mixed numerals, it is usually best to write the example vertically so the renaming can be recorded more easily. Have the child practice deciding which of several examples should be written vertically to facilitate computation and which can be computed horizontally.

2. *Use fractional parts of a unit region.* Use fractional parts to show *only* the sum, then cover or set apart the amount indicated by the known addend. The child will soon discover that it is necessary to deal with the fraction before the whole number. Have the child exchange as necessary so he can cover or set apart the amount required. Such a procedure will help him relate the problem more adequately to the operation of subtraction. However, it can become a cumbersome procedure, so choose examples carefully (An appropriate example might be $3\frac{1}{6} - 1\frac{2}{3}$.) Step-by-step, relate the activity with fractional parts to the vertical algorithm.

3. *Reteach and/or practice specific prerequisite skills.* Consider the tasks listed in Appendix D. Suggestions for instructional activities have already been described for many of these. For example, for Error Pattern A-F-3 activities are suggested which are appropriate for subtraction as well as for addition of unlike fractions. These activities are concerned with least common multiples, the identity element, and the like.

Error Pattern M-F-1

from pages 46 and 76.

How would you help a student such as Dan correct the error pattern illustrated? Are the activities you described similar to any of those below?

E. $\dfrac{3}{4} \times \dfrac{2}{3} = 89$ F. $\dfrac{4}{9} \times \dfrac{2}{5} = 200$

Note: The child's product is most unreasonable, and continued diagnosis is wise. Does the child understand the equals sign as meaning "the same"? What kind of meaning does he associate with common fractions? Does he believe that products are *always* larger numbers?

1. *Use fractional parts of unit regions.* Interpreting an example like $\frac{3}{4} \times \frac{2}{3} = ?$ as $\frac{3}{4}$ of $\frac{2}{3} = ?$, picture a rectangular region partitioned into thirds and shade two of them. This represents $\frac{2}{3}$ of one. Next, partition the unit so the child can see $\frac{3}{4}$ of the $\frac{2}{3}$. What part of the unit is shown as $\frac{3}{4}$ of $\frac{2}{3}$? Be sure the child relates the answer to the unit rather than just the $\frac{2}{3}$. Record the fact that $\frac{3}{4}$ of $\frac{2}{3} = \frac{6}{12}$ and solve other problems with drawings. Then redevelop the rule for multiplying fractions by observing a pattern among several examples completed with fractional parts of unit regions.

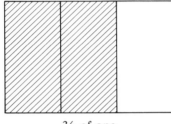

⅔ of one

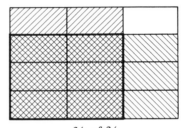

¾ of ⅔

2. *Estimate before computing*   Children often assume that the result of multiplying will be a larger number. Ask if $\frac{2}{3}$ is less than one or more than one. Is $\frac{1}{4}$ of $\frac{2}{3}$ less than one or more than one? $\frac{2}{4}$ of $\frac{2}{3}$? $\frac{3}{4}$ of $\frac{2}{3}$? Will $\frac{3}{4}$ of $\frac{2}{3}$ be less than $\frac{2}{3}$ or more than $\frac{2}{3}$? It will be helpful if the child expects his answer to be less than $\frac{2}{3}$. Of course, a child must understand fraction concepts before he can be expected to learn to estimate.

Error Pattern M-F-2

from pages 47 and 77.

What instructional activities do you suggest to help Grace correct the error pattern illustrated? See if your suggestions are among those illustrated below.

D. $\dfrac{2}{3} \times \dfrac{3}{4} = \dfrac{2}{3} \times \dfrac{4}{3} = \dfrac{8}{9}$

E. $\dfrac{5}{7} \times \dfrac{3}{8} = \dfrac{5}{7} \times \dfrac{8}{3} = \dfrac{40}{21}$

1. *Emphasize the meaning of "equals."*   *Equals* means "the same," and the expressions on either side of an equals sign should show the same number. Of course, when working with fractions, it is necessary to keep in mind the fact that a given number can be expressed with many equivalent fractions, but all equivalent fractions name the same number as labels on a number line will show. Have the child examine work that has been completed and compare the expressions on both sides of the equals sign to see if they are the same number. For example, in D the $\frac{2}{3}$ is multiplied by less than one on one side of the equals sign and by more than one on the other side.

2. *Replace computation with yes and no.*   Note that the student multiplied correctly after the second factor had been inverted. Focus on the question, "Do I invert or not?" Give the child a mixture of multiplication and division examples to write yes or no by each.

Error Pattern D-F-1

from pages 48 *and* 78.

What instructional activities do you suggest to help Linda correct the error pattern illustrated? See if your suggestions are among those described below.

E. $$\frac{4}{12} \div \frac{4}{4} = \frac{1}{3}$$ F. $$\frac{13}{20} \div \frac{5}{6} = \frac{2}{3}$$

Note: Selection of appropriate remedial activities will depend somewhat upon which algorithm for division with fractions the child was taught originally.

1. *Introduce an alternative algorithm.*   Complex fraction, common denominator, and invert and multiply are frequently taught algorithms for division with fractions. Introduce a procedure different from the one previously studied by the child.

2. *Discover a pattern.*   Introduce the invert and multiply rule by presenting a varied selection of examples complete with correct answers, e.g., $\frac{7}{12} \div \frac{3}{5} = \frac{35}{36}$. Have the child compare the problems and answers and look for a pattern among the examples. Be sure each hypothesized rule is tested by checking it against all examples in the selection. After the pattern has been found, have the child verbalize the rule and make up a few examples to solve.

3. *Estimate answers with paper strips and a number line.*   Using a number line and the measurement model for division, make a strip of paper about as long as the dividend and another about as long as the divisor. Ask how many strips the length of the divisor strip can be made from the dividend strip. For $\frac{5}{8} \div \frac{2}{5} = ?$, the answer might be "about one and a half." For example F, the estimate might be "a little less than one."

Error Pattern A-D-1

from pages 49 *and* 79.

You have described two activities for helping Harold with the difficulty illustrated below. Are either of your suggestions among those listed?

E.
$$+ \begin{array}{r} .3 \\ .5 \\ \hline .8 \end{array}$$

F.
$$+ \begin{array}{r} .7 \\ .7 \\ \hline .14 \end{array}$$

Note: Some teachers will be tempted to simply tell the child that in problems like example F the decimal point should go *between* the two digits in the sum. However, such directions only compound the problem. The child needs a greater understanding of decimal numeration and the ability to apply such knowledge. Further diagnosis is probably wise. When the addends also include units, does the child regroup tenths as units, or does he think of two separate problems—one to the right and one to the left?

$$\begin{array}{r} 6.7 \\ 8.5 \\ \hline 15.2 \end{array} \qquad \text{or} \qquad \begin{array}{r} 6.7 \\ 8.5 \\ \hline 14.12 \end{array}$$

1. *Use fraction blocks or rods.* Define one size of block as a unit. Then have the child show each addend with sets of blocks one-tenth as large as the unit. After he combines the two sets of blocks, have him exchange tenths for a unit if possible. He should compare the results of this activity with his erroneous procedure.

2. *Use a number line.* Mark units and tenths clearly on a number line and show addition with arrows. Compare the sum indicated on the number line with the sum resulting from computation.

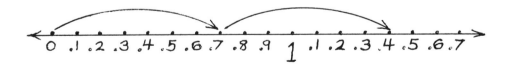

3. *Use vertically lined or cross-sectioned paper.* Theme paper can be turned 90° to use as vertically lined paper. Have the child compute using the rule that only one digit can be placed in a column. If cross-sectioned paper is used, only one digit should be written within each square.

Error Pattern M-D-1

from pages 50 *and* 79.

Below are illustrations of Marsha's error pattern in multiplication of decimals. Are the instructional activities you suggested to help this child among those described?

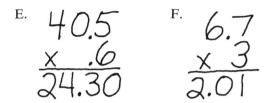

E.
$$
\begin{array}{r}
40.5 \\
\times\ \ .6 \\
\hline
24.30
\end{array}
$$

F.
$$
\begin{array}{r}
6.7 \\
\times\ 3 \\
\hline
2.01
\end{array}
$$

1. *Estimate before computing.* Use concepts like less than and more than in estimating the product before computing. For example E, a bit more than 40 is being multiplied by about a half. The product should be a bit more than 20. There is only one place where the decimal point could go if the answer is to be a bit more than 20. Similarly, in example F, 6.7 is between 6 and 7; therefore, the answer should be between 18 and 21. Again, there is only one place the decimal point can be placed for the answer to be reasonable. For 3.452 × 4.845, it can be easily seen that the product must be between 12 (i.e., 3 × 4) and 20 (i.e., 4 × 5), and there will be only one sensible place to write the decimal point.

2. *Look for a pattern.* Introduce the rule for placing the decimal point in the product by presenting a varied selection of examples complete with correct answers. Have the child compare the problems and answers and look for a pattern among the examples. Be sure the child checks his rule against all examples in the selection. When the correct rule has been established, have the child verbalize the rule and use it with a few examples he makes up himself.

Error Pattern D-D-1

from pages 51 *and* 80.

Are your suggestions for helping Ted among the suggestions listed below? He has the illustrated difficulty.

D.
$$
\begin{array}{r}
.852 \\
3\overline{\smash{)}2.57} \\
\underline{24} \\
17 \\
\underline{15} \\
2
\end{array}
$$

E.
$$
\begin{array}{r}
13.34 \\
.7\overline{\smash{)}9.35} \\
\underline{7} \\
23 \\
\underline{21} \\
25 \\
\underline{21} \\
4
\end{array}
$$

1. *Label columns on lined paper.* Turn theme paper 90° and write each column of digits between two vertical lines. Then label each column with the appropriate

place value. This may help discourage moving digits around mechanically. In example D, 2 hundredths is not the same as 2 thousandths.

2. *Study alternatives for handling remainders.* By using simple example and story problems, first show that for division of *whole* numbers there are at least three different ways to handle remainders:

a. As the amount remaining after distributing. Either a measurement or partitioning model for division can be used. The amount left over is expressed with a whole number.

$$
\begin{array}{r}
64 \\
6\overline{)387} \\
36 \\
\hline
27 \\
24 \\
\hline
3
\end{array}
$$

Answer: 64 (groups, or in each group) with 3 left over

b. As a common fraction within the quotient expressed as a mixed number. A partitioning model for division is usually used here.

$$
\begin{array}{r}
93\frac{1}{4} \\
4\overline{)373} \\
36 \\
\hline
13 \\
12 \\
\hline
1
\end{array}
$$

Answer: 93¼ for each of the 4

c. As an indicator that the quotient should be rounded up by one, often in relation to the cost of an item. For example, pencils priced 3 for 29¢ would sell for 10¢ each.

$$
\begin{array}{r}
9 \\
3\overline{)29} \\
27 \\
\hline
2
\end{array}
$$

Answer: 10¢ each

Next, consider remainders for division of decimals similarly. If the remainder in example D is viewed as the amount left over after distributing, 0.02 would remain. If it is viewed as a common fraction within the quotient, the quotient would be 0.85⅔ or 0.857.

Error Pattern S-M-1

from pages 52 *and* 81.

You have suggested instructional activities for helping Margaret, who is using the error pattern illustrated. Are any of your suggestions among those listed below?

D.
$$\begin{array}{r} \overset{5}{\cancel{6}} \text{ yards, } 1 \text{ foot} \\ -\ 2 \text{ yards, } 2 \text{ feet} \\ \hline 3 \text{ yards, } 9 \text{ feet} \end{array}$$

E.
$$\begin{array}{r} \overset{2}{\cancel{3}} \text{ quarts, } 1 \text{ cup} \\ -\ 1 \text{ quart, } 3 \text{ cups} \\ \hline 1 \text{ quart, } 8 \text{ cups} \end{array}$$

1. *Use measuring devices.*   First, have the child show the minuend with measuring devices. In example D it could be shown with yardsticks and foot rulers. Then have the child take away as much length (volume, etc.) as is suggested by the subtrahend. In the process it will be necessary to exchange. Be sure to point out that the exchanges are not always with ones and a ten; many other kinds of exchanges occur with measurement situations.

2. *Regroup in many different number bases.*   Use multibase blocks, place-value charts, or sticks and bundles of sticks to learn to regroup in different number bases. A game-rule orientation in which the rule for exchanging changes from game to game may help the child generalize the regrouping pattern. For base 4 games and activities the rule would be "Exchange a 4 for ones"; in base 12 games the rule would be "Exchange a 12 for ones," etc. Follow such activities with computation involving measurement and emphasize that the regrouping is similar to that encountered in other number bases.

3. *Identify number base relationships.*   Have the child determine the number base relationship which obtains in specific computation situations involving measurement.

Conclusion

Diagnosis and remediation are continuous processes. Diagnosis continues during remedial activity as you observe the child at work and note patterns. Remediation also continues, for even when the child appears able to use correct procedures, you need to keep a close watch to make sure he consistently uses them.

As you continue your work with a child, make sure he is aware of his strengths. Help him take note of the progress he makes. Proceed in very small steps, if necessary, to insure successful experiences. It is important that your sessions with the child be varied and include games and puzzles which are fun for the child. Remedial teaching should first of all build upon the child's strengths. As the child gains confidence and as the activities he associates with mathematics become enjoyable, he will be much more open to your continued efforts to remediate specific difficulties.

Selected References

A. *References Focusing on Diagnostic Tasks*

Ablewhite, R. C. *Mathematics and the Less Able*. London: Heinemann Educational Books, Ltd., 1969. Chapter one includes examples of children's work from British schools along with a discussion of the errors exemplified.

Arthur, Lee E. "Diagnosis of Disabilities in Arithmetic Essentials." *The Mathematics Teacher* 43 (May 1950):197–202. The author reports a study of the abilities of high school students with reference to the "essentials" of arithmetic. Remedial teaching of these essentials is recommended in all high school mathematics classes.

Brownell, William A. "The Evaluation of Learning in Arithmetic." *Arithmetic in General Education*. 16th Yearbook of the National Council of Teachers of Mathematics. Washington, D. C.: NCTM., 1941, pp. 225–67. A comprehensive and amazingly current discussion of the topic.

Brueckner, Leo J. *Diagnostic and Remedial Teaching in Arithmetic*. Philadelphia: The John C. Winston Co., 1930. A classic in the area of diagnosis and treatment of disabilities in mathematics, much of this book is based upon early studies of the errors pupils make in computation.

Brueckner, Leo J., and Bond, Guy L. *The Diagnosis and Treatment of Learning Difficulties*. New York: Appleton-Century-Crofts, 1955. Chapter eight deals specifically with diagnosis of learning difficulties in arithmetic.

Buswell G. T., and John, Lenore. *Manual of Directions for Use with Diagnostic Chart for Individual Difficulties, Fundamental Processes in Arithmetic*. Bloomington, Ill.: Public School Publishing Co., n.d. Most of this manual from the 1920s consists of detailed illustrations of children's work habits for computation with whole numbers. Many error patterns are included.

Caldwell, Edward. "Group Diagnosis and Standardized Achievement Tests." *The Arithmetic Teacher* 12 (February 1965):123–25. The author outlines steps for the classroom teacher to take in the use of achievement test results.

Callahan, Leroy G., and Robinson, Mary L. "Task-Analysis Procedures in Mathematics Instruction of Achievers & Underachievers." *School Science and Mathematics* 73

(October 1973):578–84. The authors report research suggesting that, when the task-analysis procedures of Gagné are combined with meaningful mastery learning of subordinate tasks in a hierarchy, learning of a mathematical task can be quite effective.

Cox, L. S. "Diagnosing and Remediating Systematic Errors in Addition and Subtraction Computations." *The Arithmetic Teacher* 22 (February 1975):151–57. Cox emphasizes that teachers must look for patterns in the work they collect from pupils having difficulty with computation. He describes three categories of errors which can be noted.

Dahle, Casper O. "The Verbal Thought and Overt Behavior of Children During Their Learning of Long Division." *Journal of Experimental Education* 9 (September 1940): 1–8. Dahle reports detailed observations of children learning to divide. The study is rather unique and includes electrodermal responses.

Dodd, Carol A.; Jones, Graham A., and Lamb, Charles E., "Diagnosis and Remediation of Pupil Errors: An Exploratory Study," *School Science and Mathematics,* 75:270-76 (March 1975). The authors compare two different programs of instruction to see which is more effective for preparing elementary teachers to identify patterns of error and prescribe remediation. They conclude that the ability to diagnose is largely a function of reasoning ability and teacher education should stress remediation.

Dutton, Wilbur H. *Evaluating Pupils' Understanding of Arithmetic.* Englewood Cliffs, N. J.: Prentice-Hall, 1964. This book emphasizes procedures for assessing pupil understanding of mathematical ideas as opposed to skill acquisition alone.

Epstein, Marion G. "Testing in Mathematics: Why? What? How?" *The Arithmetic Teacher* 15 (April 1968):311–19. Included in this article is the ETS classification system for test questions which can be used for relating test items to levels of thinking.

Flournoy, Frances; Brandt, Dorothy; and McGregor, Johnnie. "Pupil Understanding of the Numeration System." *The Arithmetic Teacher* 10 (February 1963):88–92. The authors describe a test for pupil understanding of our numeration system and the results of a test administration. The need for varied exercises in instruction is emphasized.

Gagné, Robert M. "Learning and Proficiency in Mathematics." *The Mathematics Teacher* 56 (December 1963):620–26. Gagné describes a method of analyzing desired pupil behaviors into subordinant behaviors.

Gibb, E. Glenadine. "Children's Thinking in the Process of Subtraction." *Journal of Experimental Education* 25 (September 1956):71–80. Gibb's study analyzes children's thoughts while solving problems involving the process of subtraction. Interviews were used for data gathering.

Glennon, Vincent J., and Wilson, John W. "Diagnostic-Prescriptive Teaching." *The Slow Learner in Mathematics.* 35th Yearbook of the National Council of Teachers of Mathematics. Washington, D. C.: NCTM, 1972, pp. 282–318. Within the context of a larger view of curriculum and methods variables, the authors present a model for cognitive diagnosis and prescription. A content taxonomy is related to behavioral indicators and kinds of psychological learning products. Procedures for diagnostic-prescriptive teaching are discussed and illustrated; sample lesson plans are included.

Grafft, William. "A Study of Behavioral Performances within the Structure of Multiplication." *The Arithmetic Teacher* 17 (April 1970):335–37. The author describes the kinds of tasks a child should be able to do in an interview if he understands the operation of multiplication and its place within mathematical structures.

Gray, Roland F. "An Approach to Evaluating Arithmetic Understandings." *The Arithmetic Teacher* 13 (March 1966):187–91. Gray shows how the individual interview can be used as a data-gathering technique even for research purposes.

Hammitt, Helen. "Evaluating and Reteaching Slow Learners." *The Arithmetic Teacher* 14 (January 1967):40–41. Hammitt proposes a plan for children to regularly evaluate their own skills in computation.

Homan, Doris R. "The Child with a Learning Disability in Arithmetic." *The Arithmetic Teacher* 18 (March 1970):199–203. Homan is concerned with the diagnostic-remedial process, particularly where children appear unable to learn arithmetic. Perceptual skills, motor disinhibition, perseverance, language, and reasoning are discussed; and a few remedial techniques are suggested.

Jansson, Lars C. "Judging Mathematical Statements in the Classroom." *The Arithmetic Teacher* 18 (November 1971):463–66. The author alerts us to the way children often interpret statements in the mathematics lesson and suggests types of judgments teachers need to make when evaluating such statements.

Koenker, Robert H. "Certain Characteristic Differences Between Excellent and Poor Achievers in Two-Figure Division." *Journal of Educational Research* 35 (April 1942): 578–86. This is the report of a study comparing specific concepts and skills possessed by high achievers and low achievers in two-digit division.

Lankford, Francis G., Jr. *Some Computational Strategies of Seventh Grade Pupils.* U. S. Department of Health, Education, and Welfare, Office of Education, National Center for Educational Research and Development (Regional Research Program) and The Center for Advanced Study, University of Virginia, October 1972 (Project number 2-C-013, Grant number OEG-3-72-0035). A comprehensive report of a study of errors in computation in which data were gathered through individual "diagnostic interviews." The study was limited to operations on whole numbers and fractions, with a few items involving comparisons among fractions.

——————————. "What Can a Teacher Learn About a Pupil's Thinking through Oral Interviews?" *The Arithmetic Teacher* 21 (January 1974):26–32. This is a brief report drawn from Lankford's larger monograph.

Luriya, A. R. "On the Pathology of Computational Operations." In *Soviet Studies in the Psychology of Learning and Teaching Mathematics*, Vol. I, edited by Jeremy Kilpatrick and Izaak Wirsup. School Mathematics Study Group and the University of Chicago, 1969, pp. 37–74. In an effort to trace the difficulties peculiar to the process of mastering number and computation. Luriya reports research with individuals where there has been a breakdown of the number concept and of computational operations because of some form of brain disease.

O'Brien, Thomas C., and Richard, June V. "Interviews to Assess Number Knowledge." *The Arithmetic Teacher* 18 (May 1971):322–26. The authors describe five tasks presented to children to assess their knowledge of counting and simple addition and subtraction situations. Children's responses are classified and related to Piaget's observations of children.

Peck, Donald M., and Jencks, Stanley M. "What the Tests Don't Tell." *The Arithmetic Teacher* 21 (January 1974):54–56. The authors illustrate the limitations of paper-and-pencil tests, especially with reference to equivalent fractions.

Reisman, Fredricka, K. *A Guide to the Diagnostic Teaching of Arithmetic.* Columbus, Ohio: Charles E. Merrill Publishing Co., 1972. Reisman relates the writings of several psychologists to the diagnostic teaching of arithmetic. Sample diagnostic tools are provided for the teacher. Case studies are included.

Roberts, Gerhard H. "The Failure Strategies of Third Grade Arithmetic Pupils." *The Arithmetic Teacher* 15 (May 1968):442–46. Roberts reports a study in which computational errors are classified within four error categories and compared with grade-level scores on an achievement test.

Shafer, Dale M. "Multiplication Mastery Via the Tape Recorder." *The Arithmetic Teacher* 17 (November 1970):581–82. The author describes a procedure for scoring response sheets for drills or self-checks administered by a tape recorder, a procedure which is efficient and provides diagnostic feedback.

Swart, William L. "Evaluation of Mathematics Instruction in the Elementary Classroom." *The Arithmetic Teacher* 21 (January 1974):7–13. The author illustrates the limitations of paper-and pencil tests, particularly with reference to goals of instruction.

Walbesser, Henry H. *Constructing Behavioral Objectives.* College Park, Md.: Bureau of Educational Research and Field Services, College of Education, University of Maryland, 1968. Training in the construction of behavioral objectives and learning hierarchies is presented in a semi-programmed format.

Weaver, J. Fred. "Big Dividends from Little Interviews." *The Arithmetic Teacher* 2 (April 1955):40–47. Weaver discusses the values of individual interviews and illustrates the kind of information which can thereby be obtained from children. The use of such data while planning future instruction is also illustrated.

——————. "Evaluation and the Classroom Teacher." In *Mathematics Education.* Sixty-ninth Yearbook of the National Society for the Study of Education, Part I, edited by E. G. Begle. Chicago: The University of Chicago Press, 1970, pp. 335–66. A model is described which relates areas of mathematical content, levels of desired behavior, and techniques for observing instructional outcomes.

West, Tommie A. "Diagnosing Pupil Errors: Looking for Patterns." *The Arithmetic Teacher* 18 (November 1971):467–69. West illustrates and discusses error patterns in written computation and urges critical examination of children's work.

B. *References Focusing on Remedial Tasks*

Anderson, Rosemary C. "Suggestions from Research — Fractions." *The Arithmetic Teacher* 16 (February 1969):131–35. This summary provides useful guidance for the remediation of difficulties with fractions.

Ando, Masue, and Hitoshi, Ikeda. "Learning Multiplication Facts — More Than Drill." *The Arithmetic Teacher* 18 (October 1971):366–69. The authors suggest varied activities to help children understand and remember the basic multiplication facts.

Arnold, William R. "Computation Made Interesting." *The Arithmetic Teacher* 18 (May 1971):347–50. The author describes several pattern-seeking and pattern-extending activities which can be used for practice with the basic facts of arithmetic in place of an emphasis on worksheets.

Arnsdorf, Edward E. "A Game for Reviewing Basic Facts of Arithmetic." *The Arithmetic Teacher* 19 (November 1972):589–90. Arnsdorf describes a card game for practice recalling basic facts for all four operations.

Ashlock, Robert B. "Teaching the Basic Facts: Three Classes of Activities." *The Arithmetic Teacher* 18 (October 1971):359–64. The author illustrates three kinds of instructional activities which children need if they are to learn the basic facts of arithmetic.

Batarseh, Gabriel J. "Addition for the Slow Learner." *The Arithmetic Teacher* 21 (December 1974):714–15. An alternative algorithm for addition of whole numbers is described.

Beardslee, Edward C.; Gau, Gerald E.; and Heimer, Ralph T. "Teaching for Generaliza-tion: An Array Approach to Equivalent Fractions." *The Arithmetic Teacher* 20 (November 1973):591–99. The authors illustrate activity cards which can help children make generalizations about equivalent fractions by observing specially constructed arrays.

Beardsley, Leah Mildred. *1001 Uses of the Hundred Square: Activities and Ideas for Teaching Mathematics.* West Nyack, New York: Parker Publishing Company, 1973. The author has compiled a very useful set of suggestions for instructional activities, categorized by content (e.g., multiplication).

Braunfeld, Peter, and Wolfe, Martin. "Fractions for Low Achievers." *The Arithmetic Teacher* 13 (December 1966):647–55. The authors describe a novel approach to fractions involving hooking up stretching and shrinking machines.

Broadbent, Frank W. " 'Contig': A Game to Practice and Sharpen Skills and Facts in the Four Fundamental Operations." *The Arithmetic Teacher* 19 (May 1972): 388–90. The game which is described is a board game that can be easily made and varied according to the needs of participants.

Brownell, William A. "The Progressive Nature of Learning in Mathematics." *The Mathematics Teacher* 37 (April 1944):147–57. A most helpful article in which Brownell discusses selected weaknesses in mathematics instruction and describes the kinds of activities which may be appropriate at different stages of learning.

Brownell, William A., and Chazal, Charlotte B. "The Effects of Premature Drill in Third-Grade Arithmetic." In *Current Research in Elementary School Mathematics,* edited by R. B. Ashlock and W. L. Herman, Jr. New York: The Macmillan Co., 1970, pp. 170–88. A report of a classic study in mathematics education which examines the effects of practice on a child's quantitative thinking with respect to the basic facts of arithmetic. The interview is used as a data-gathering technique, and representative interviews are reported in detail.

Cacha, Frances B. "Understanding Multiplication and Division of Multidigit Numbers." *The Arithmetic Teacher* 19 (May 1972):349–55. Cacha describes how children can be helped to understand the algorithms through the use of arrays made of graph paper.

Callahan, Leroy. "Remedial Work with Underachieving Children." *The Arithmetic Teacher* 9 (March 1962):138–40. Callahan describes a three-month individual diagnostic and remedial program which significantly reduced the underachievement of participants.

Cohen, Louis S. "The Board Stretcher: A Model to Introduce Factors, Primes, Composites, and Multiplication by a Fraction." *The Arithmetic Teacher* 20 (December 1973): 649–56. Board stretching and shrinking machines are used for an approach to renaming fractions.

Dienes, Zoltan P. "Some Basic Processes Involved in Mathematics Learning." *Research in Mathematics Education.* Washington, D. C.: National Council of Teachers of Mathematics, 1967, pp. 21–34. In much of this essay Dienes focuses upon the abstracting and generalizing of concepts by children and the role played by language in learning mathematics.

Dilley, Clyde A., and Rucker, Walter E. "Division with Common and Decimal Fractional Numbers." *The Arithmetic Teacher* 17 (May 1970):438–41. An alternative ap-proach for division of rationals is described.

DiSpigno, Joseph. "Division Isn't That Hard." *The Arithmetic Teacher* 18 (October 1971):373–77. The author illustrates a method for helping children understand the division algorithm, a method which uses only paper and pencil.

Fishback, Sylvia. "Times Without Tears." *The Arithmetic Teacher* 21 (March 1974): 200–1. A teacher describes her successful use of a matrix and distributivity for teaching the basic multiplication facts.

Fulkerson, Elbert. "Adding by Tens." *The Arithmetic Teacher* 10 (March 1963):139–40. The author describes an addition algorithm useful as an alternative to the standard algorithm.

Gosman, Howard Y. "Mastering the Basic Facts with Dice." *The Arithmetic Teacher* 20 (May 1973):330–31. The author describes simple games for addition and multiplication using only dice.

Gray, Roland F. "An Experiment in the Teaching of Introductory Multiplication." *The Arithmetic Teacher* 12 (March 1965):199–203. From his study Gray concludes that knowledge of the distributive property appears to help children proceed independently when solving untaught multiplication combinations.

Gunderson, Agnes G. "Thought-Patterns of Young Children in Learning Multiplication and Division." *Elementary School Journal* 55 (April 1955):453–61. Observations of varied responses of children to multiplication and division problems suggest that second grade is not too early to introduce such problems, but instruction should proceed cautiously from concrete materials to abstract symbols.

Hannon, Herbert. "All About Division with Rational Numbers — Variations on a Theme." *School Science and Mathematics* 71 (June 1971):501–7. The author illustrates several different algorithms for dividing with fractions.

Harvey, Lois F., and Kyte, George C. "Zero Difficulties in Multiplication." *The Arithmetic Teacher* 12 (January 1965):45–50. The authors report the results of an institutional program which isolated specific errors involving zero in multiplication of whole numbers and included remedial teaching which appeared to be effective.

Hawthorne, Frank S. "Hand-held Calculators: Help or Hindrance?" *The Arithmetic Teacher* 20 (December 1973):671–72. The author discusses the effect of small calculators on the arithmetic program and states some cautions.

Heckman, M. Jane: "They All Add Up." *The Arithmetic Teacher* 21 (April 1974): 287–89. Games for practicing the basic facts of arithmetic are described.

Heddens, James W., and Hynes, Michael. "Division of Fractional Numbers." *The Arithmetic Teacher* 16 (February 1969):99–103. The authors show how previously learned concepts and the use of varied exemplars can help children understand division of fractional numbers.

Henry, Boyd. "Zero, the Troublemaker." *The Arithmetic Teacher* 16 (May 1969): 365–67. Henry focuses on the difficult problem of zero as a divisor.

Hutchings, Barton. "Low-stress Subtraction." *The Arithmetic Teacher* 22 (March 1975): 226–32. Hutchings describes a subtraction procedure which has been demonstrated to be an especially effective remedial tool.

Ikeda, Hitoshi, and Ando, Masue. "A New Algorithm for Subtraction?" *The Arithmetic Teacher* 21 (December 1974):716–19. The authors suggest an alternative to the conventional decomposition algorithm.

Kevra, Barbara; Brey, Rita; and Schimmel, Barbara. "Success for Slower Learners, or Rx: Relax . . . and Play." *The Arithmetic Teacher* 19 (May 1972):335–43. The authors present a variety of ideas for practicing the basic facts of arithmetic.

Kratzer, Richard Oren. "A Comparison of Initially Teaching Division Employing the Distributive and Greenwood Algorithm with the Aid of a Manipulative Material." *Dissertation Abstracts Intl.* 32A (April 1972):5672. Kratzer reports research comparing a repetitive subtraction-division algorithm with a partitioning distributive method. The latter was more effective when pupils were presented unfamiliar verbal problems.

Marion, Charles F. "How to Get Subtraction Into the Game." *The Arithmetic Teacher* 17 (February 1970):169–70. The author describes a variation for board games which will give children additional practice with simple addition and subtraction.

Metzner, Seymour, and Sharp, Richard M. "Cardematics I — Using Playing Cards As Reinforcers and Motivators in Basic Operations." *The Arithmetic Teacher* 21 (May 1974):419–21. The authors describe several games for practicing the basic facts of arithmetic, games using regular playing cards.

Molinoski, Marie: "Facto." *The Arithmetic Teacher* 21 (April 1974):321–22. The author describes a game for practice in relating fractions, decimals, and percents.

Phillips, Jo. " 'Basic Laws' for Young Children." *The Arithmetic Teacher* 12 (November 1965):525–32. Phillips cautions against rote learning of vocabulary and illustrates careful teaching of the properties of whole number operations.

Pincus, Morris. "Addition and Subtraction Fraction Algorisms." *The Arithmetic Teacher* 16 (February 1969):141–42. The author suggests an alternative designed to eliminate some of the more common careless errors.

Quast, W. G. "On Computation and Drill." *The Arithmetic Teacher* 16 (December 1969): 627-30. Quast illustrates the dangers to be avoided when working with children on computation.

Rinker, Ethel. "Eight-ring Circus: A Variation in the Teaching of Counting and Place Value." *The Arithmetic Teacher* 19 (March 1972):209–18. The use of several homemade exemplars is illustrated for the teaching of numeration.

Scott, Lloyd. "A Study of Teaching Division through the Use of Two Algorithms." *School Science and Mathematics* 63 (December 1963):739–52. The author argues for teaching both measurement and partitioning division to children.

Smith, C. Winston, Jr. "The Witch's Best Game." *The Arithmetic Teacher* 13 (December 1966):683–84. The author describes a game setting in which children focus on renaming the minuend in subtraction involving regrouping.

————. "Tiger-bite Cards and Blank Arrays." *The Arithmetic Teacher* 21 (December 1974):679-83. Smith illustrates a clever use of arrays for relating multiplication and division and for introducing the subtractive division algorithm.

Swart, William L. "Teaching the Division-by-Subtraction Process." *The Arithmetic Teacher* 19 (January 1972):71–76. Swart anticipates many of the questions children have as they are introduced to this algorithm.

Tucker, Benny F. "The Division Algorithm." *The Arithmetic Teacher* 20 (December 1973):639–46. Tucker describes how the division algorithm can be introduced using the partitive model and a variety of exemplars.

Vest, Floyd. "Model Switching Found in Lessons in Subtraction in the Elementary Grades." *School Science and Mathematics* 70 (May 1970):407–10. Vest cautions against the practice of confusing children by unnecessarily switching models in the midst of an instructional sequence.

Zweng, Marilyn J. "The Fourth Operation is Not Fundamental." *The Arithmetic Teacher* 19 (December 1972):623–29. Zweng discusses the role of division of whole numbers in problem solving, and considers implications for teaching division computation.

Additional Children's Papers

On the following pages are brief excerpts from the written work of children using erroneous computational procedures. Practice the skill of identifying error patterns by finding the erroneous procedure in each of these papers. Briefly describe each error pattern, then check the key on page 134 if you wish.

Paper A

$$\begin{array}{r} 35 \\ +28 \\ \hline 18 \end{array} \qquad \begin{array}{r} 24 \\ +17 \\ \hline 14 \end{array} \qquad \begin{array}{r} 43 \\ +26 \\ \hline 15 \end{array}$$

Description of Pattern _____

_____

Paper B

$$\begin{array}{r} 47 \\ -3 \\ \hline 14 \end{array} \qquad \begin{array}{r} 65 \\ -2 \\ \hline 43 \end{array} \qquad \begin{array}{r} 78 \\ -4 \\ \hline 34 \end{array}$$

Description of Pattern _____

_____

Paper C

$$\begin{array}{r} 62 \\ -5 \\ \hline 75 \end{array}$$ $$\begin{array}{r} 84 \\ -8 \\ \hline 67 \end{array}$$ $$\begin{array}{r} 51 \\ -3 \\ \hline 84 \end{array}$$

Description of Pattern _____

_____

Paper D

$$\begin{array}{r} 65 \\ -29 \\ \hline 46 \end{array}$$ $$\begin{array}{r} 437 \\ -84 \\ \hline 453 \end{array}$$ $$\begin{array}{r} 226 \\ -173 \\ \hline 153 \end{array}$$

Description of Pattern _____

_____

Paper E

$$\begin{array}{r} 874 \\ -247 \\ \hline 527 \end{array}$$ $$\begin{array}{r} 493 \\ -156 \\ \hline 237 \end{array}$$ $$\begin{array}{r} 762 \\ -418 \\ \hline 244 \end{array}$$

Description of Pattern _____

_____

Paper F

$$\begin{array}{r} 52 \\ -27 \\ \hline 30 \end{array}$$ $$\begin{array}{r} 615 \\ -142 \\ \hline 503 \end{array}$$ $$\begin{array}{r} 322 \\ -156 \\ \hline 200 \end{array}$$

Description of Pattern _____

_____

Paper G

$31-7=\underline{22}$　　$23-4=\underline{13}$

$42-5=\underline{33}$　　$51-3=\underline{46}$

Description of Pattern _____

_____

Paper H

```
  539      457      928
 - 83     - 65     - 34
  206      102      524
  351      211      615
  557      313     1139
```

Description of Pattern _____

_____

Paper I

```
   98       37       56
 × 13      ×24      × 32
  294      148      112
   98       74      168
  392      222      280
```

Description of Pattern _____

_____

Paper J

```
  723      368      475
 ×   6     ×   6    ×   9
 4338     1978     3745
```

Description of Pattern _____

_____

Paper K

$$
\begin{array}{r}
{}^{1}{}_{3} \\
36 \\
\times\ 25 \\
\hline
180 \\
102 \\
\hline
1200
\end{array}
\qquad
\begin{array}{r}
{}^{3}{}_{2} \\
78 \\
\times\ 43 \\
\hline
234 \\
332 \\
\hline
3554
\end{array}
\qquad
\begin{array}{r}
{}^{1}{}_{3} \\
65 \\
\times\ 37 \\
\hline
455 \\
225 \\
\hline
2705
\end{array}
$$

Description of Pattern _____

_____

Paper L

$$
\begin{array}{r}
{}^{4} \\
37 \\
\times\ 6 \\
\hline
72
\end{array}
\qquad
\begin{array}{r}
{}^{1} \\
85 \\
\times\ 3 \\
\hline
95
\end{array}
\qquad
\begin{array}{r}
{}^{2} \\
25 \\
\times\ 4 \\
\hline
40
\end{array}
$$

Description of Pattern _____

_____

Paper M

$$
\begin{array}{r}
436 \\
\times\ 25 \\
\hline
2180 \\
872 \\
\hline
6660
\end{array}
\qquad
\begin{array}{r}
379 \\
\times\ 42 \\
\hline
758 \\
1516 \\
\hline
15618
\end{array}
\qquad
\begin{array}{r}
754 \\
\times 268 \\
\hline
6032 \\
4524 \\
1508 \\
\hline
111612
\end{array}
$$

Description of Pattern _____

_____

Paper N

$$
\begin{array}{r}
132 \\
\times\ 6 \\
\hline
1512
\end{array}
\qquad
\begin{array}{r}
358 \\
\times\ 4 \\
\hline
1522
\end{array}
\qquad
\begin{array}{r}
492 \\
\times\ 7 \\
\hline
3264
\end{array}
$$

Paper O $\frac{2}{3}+\frac{1}{4}=37$ $\frac{5}{6}+\frac{1}{2}=68$

Description of Pattern _____

_____

Paper P $\frac{1}{3}+\frac{2}{9}=\frac{3}{9}$ $\frac{3}{4}+\frac{3}{2}=\frac{6}{4}$

Description of Pattern _____

_____

Paper Q

$4\frac{2}{3}\times\frac{1}{4}=4\frac{2}{12}$ $6\frac{3}{4}\times\frac{2}{3}=6\frac{6}{12}$

Description of Pattern _____

_____

Key for Additional Children's Papers

A. The sum of all digits is determined, regardless of place value.

B. The minuend is subtracted from both the ones and the tens.

C. The child counts backwards to determine the missing addend but reverses the digits when recording the number.

D. The child is not remembering to subtract one ten (or one hundred) when he regroups.

E. The child is subtracting one hundred from the minuend even when he has not regrouped.

F. "Seven from two is nothing."

G. The minuend is rounded down to the nearest decade, then the known addend is subtracted. Finally, the number of units in the minuend is subtracted.

H. Using the computational sequence associated with multiplication, the child is comparing digits and recording each difference. As is true for multiplication, addition precedes the final answer.

I. The second partial product is placed incorrectly.

J. In regrouping, one is always added regardless of the number required.

K. When multiplying by the tens digit, both crutch figures are used.

L. For the tens, the child just adds without multiplying first.

M. The partial products are "subtracted" by finding differences.

N. After adding the number of tens to be remembered, the *tens* digit is recorded (in the tens place!) and the units digit is "carried."

O. The numerators are added and recorded (as tens), then the denominators are added and recorded to the right (as ones).

P. The numerators are added and recorded as the new numerator. The larger denominator is used as the new denominator because the smaller denominator "will go into" the larger denominator.

Q. The common fractions are multiplied, with the result affixed to the whole number.

The Nature of Wrong Answers[1]

Whole Numbers

There were 2173 possible answers to the thirteen exercises with whole numbers by the 176 pupils interviewed. . . . Of these possible answers 1658 (76%) were right; 449 (21%) were wrong; and 66 (3%) were omitted. . . .

Addition

1. Many combinations were recalled incorrectly in addition, as in "9 + 8 = 18, + 1 = 19 and 8 is 27," or "7 × 8 = 63," or "8 × 5 = 35," or "7 × 8 = 48." The same was true in each of the other operations.

2. When counting was used pupils often lost count of the counting as in counting 9 on to 17 in 17 + 9 and getting 25, or in "7 × 8 = 57 (7 × 5 = 35; 7 × 6 = 42; 7 × 7 = 49; 50, 51, 52, 53, 54, 55, 57, 57)."

3. Many pupils failed to add the carried digit even when it was written above the top digit in the column to the left.

4. Sometimes the wrong digit was carried from the sum of one column to the next as in "2 + 3 = 5, + 9 = 14, + 7 = 21, put down the 2 and carry 1."

5. Intending to add, a pupil may have, in fact, multiplied as in "7 + 2 is 14, + 5 is 19, + 2 is 21, + 4 is 25."

Subtraction

6. Some pupils intended to subtract but in fact divided as in 93 − 32, "2 from 3 is 1; 3 from 9 is 3."

7. A wrong order was often used in subtraction as in 86 − 49, a pupil would say "9 minus 6 is 3; 8 − 4 is 4" or "9 from 6 leaves 3 and 4 from 8 leaves 4" or in 708 − 329 a pupil said "9 from 8 is 1; 2 from 0 is 0; 7 from 3 is 4."

[1]From Francis G. Lankford, Jr., *Some Computational Strategies of Seventh Grade Pupils,* U. S. Department of Health, Education, and Welfare, Office of Education, National Center for Educational Research and Development (Regional Research Program) and The Center for Advanced Study, The University of Virginia, October 1972 (Project number 2-C-013, Grant number OEG-3-72-0035), pp. 27–33.

8. A pupil would think to borrow to increase a digit but not reduce the digit from which borrowed, as in 86 − 49 "16 − 9 = 7 [counting]; 8 − 4 = 4."

9. When borrowing, as in 708 − 329, a pupil might borrow twice, once to make 0 a 10, and again to make 8 an 18, leaving the 7 as 5.

10. Some pupils borrowed from the tens column only, when they should have borrowed from both tens and hundreds columns, as in 708 − 329, rewrote 708 as 7-9-18, then "18 from 9 is 9; 9 from 2 is 7; 7 from 4 is 3."

11. Other pupils borrowed from the hundreds column only and rewrote the tens digit incorrectly. As in 708 − 329; rewritten as 6-10-18. Then 18 − 9 = 9; 10 − 2 = 8; 6 − 3 = 3.

12. The minuend was rewritten simply by affixing ones where needed, as in 708 − 329 which became 7-10-18 for 708 and the answer was 18 − 9 = 9; 10 − 2 = 8; 7 − 3 = 4.

Multiplication

13. The ones digit was multiplied by the ones digit and the tens digit by the tens digit only, as in 19 × 20 = _____, rewritten as 19, then "0 × 9 = 0 and 2 × 1 = 2"
$$\times\,20$$
answer 20; or 58 "5 × 8 = 40; 7 × 5 = 35, + 4 = 39. Written as a single
$$\times\,75$$
product 390.

14. The carried number was not included in the partial product, as in 19 × 20 = _____, rewritten as 19 , then "0 × 9 = 0; 0 × 1 = 0; 2 × 9 = 18; 2 × 1 = 2."
$$\times\,20$$

Throughout the remaining pages of this report a hyphen or hyphens after a numeral indicate an indentation in the arrangement of a partial product. For example, partial products 1824, 000, and 1520- were arranged by the pupil this way

$$\begin{array}{r} 1824 \\ 000 \\ 1520 \\ \hline 17024 \end{array}$$

or partial products 1824, 000- 1520--were arranged this way

$$\begin{array}{r} 1824 \\ 000 \\ 1520 \\ \hline 153824 \end{array}$$

15. Place value of partial products was confused as in 19   "0 × 9 = 0; 0 × 1 = 0;
$$\begin{array}{r} 20 \\ \hline 3800 \end{array}$$
2 × 9 = 18; 2 × 1 = 2, + 1 = 3." Or in 304   "6 × 304 = 1824; 0 × 304 = 000;
$$506$$
5 × 304 = 1520- for sum 17024.

16. The wrong product was written when one factor was 0, as in 19 × 20 = _____; "0 × 9 = 9; 0 × 1 = 1; 2 × 9 = 18; 2 + 1 = 2, + 1 = 3." Pupil wrote 38- under 19 for sum of 399.

17. A multiplication fact was recalled incorrectly as 7 × 8 = 54, in 58 × 75   "8 × 5 = 40; 5 × 5 = 25, +4 = 29; 7 × 8 = 54; 7 × 5 = 35, + 4 = 40." Then 290 + 404- = 4330.

18. One of the digits in the multiplier was not used in finding the product, as in 304
$$\times 506$$
   only two partial products 6 × 304 = 1824; 5 × 304 = 1520-. Sum 17024.

19. Partial products were found correctly but errors were made in adding them, as in 58
$$\times 75$$
   5 × 58 = 290; 7 × 58 = 406- for sum 4360, said "9 + 6 = 16" in adding partial products.

Division

20. A remainder was interpreted wrongly as in 27/$\overline{81}$ 81 ÷ 27 = 3; 3 × 27 = 81; 81 − 81 = 0; "27 won't go into 0, so answer is 30"; or in 48/$\overline{93}$ "48 goes into 93 one time; 1 × 48 = 48; 93 − 48 = 45; 48 can't go into 45; put 0 up; 45 − 0 = 45" for answer 10 R45.

21. Long division was confused with short division as in 27/$\overline{81}$ "2 goes into 8 four times; 2 × 4 = 8. Then 81 − 8- = 01; 2 won't go into 1" so answer is 4 R1. Or in 48/93 "4 goes into 9 two times; 4 × 2 = 8; 9 − 8 = 1; bring down 3; 8 goes into 13 one time; 8 × 1 = 8; 13 − 8 = 5" answer 21 R5.

22. Quotient digit was multiplied by the divisor incorrectly, as in 74/$\overline{6484}$ "8 × 74 = 572" (8 × 4 = 32; 8 × 7 = 54, + 3 = 57).

23. Errors were made in repeated multiplications to find quotient digit, as in 74/$\overline{6484}$ decided 74 goes into 648 seven times, then 7 × 74 = 658 (thought 7 × 4 = 28 and 7 × 7 = 56, + 7 = 63).

24. Derived an answer before operation was complete, as in 74/$\overline{6484}$ "74 goes into 648, eight times; 648 − 592 = 56," so answer is 8 R56.

25. By repeated multiplication tried incorrectly to derive entire quotient instead of one digit at a time ,as in 74/$\overline{6484}$ multiplied 74 by 12, by 24, by 52 and by 61. Chose 52 for quotient "because 3848 is closest to 6484"; then 6484 − 3848 = 2636. Placed 2734 (incorrect product of 74 × 61) under 2636. Then 2636 − 2734 = 102. Answer 5251 R102.

26. Place value was handled incorrectly in the quotient, as in 15/$\overline{7590}$ "15 goes into 75 five times 75 − 75 = 0; bring down your 9; 15 won't go into 9 so bring down 0; 6 × 15 = 90" so answer is 56. Or 15 into 75 five times; 75 − 75 = 0 "15 won't go into 0 so bring down 9; 15 won't go into 9 so bring down 0; 15 into 90 goes 6 times; 90 − 90 = 0; 15 into 0 zero times" so answer is 560.

Fractions

There were 2640 possible answers to the sixteen exercises in computation with fractions by the 176 pupils interviewed..... Of these possible answers, 924 (35%) were right; 865 (33%) were wrong; and 851 (32%) were omitted. . . .

Addition

1. A prevalent practice was to add numerators and place the sum over one of the denominators or over a common denominator, as in ¾ + ½ = ⁸⁄₄ "5 + 3 = 8. You don't add the bottom numbers because 2 will go into 4."

2. The most prevalent practice in adding fractions was to add numerators for the numerator of the sum and the same for the denominators, as in $\frac{3}{4} + \frac{1}{2} = \frac{4}{6}$ or $\frac{3}{8} + \frac{7}{8} = \frac{10}{16}$.

3. Many errors were made as pupils undertook to write equivalent fractions with common denominators, as in $\frac{3}{4} + \frac{1}{2} = $ _____; chose 4 as C.D. Then, for $\frac{3}{4}$, "4 times 1 equals 4 and 1 + 3 is 4," so $\frac{4}{4}$; for $\frac{1}{2}$ "2 × 2 = 4 and 4 × 5 = 20," so $\frac{20}{4}$; or $\frac{8}{8}$ for $\frac{7}{8}$ ("8 into 8 one time and 1 + 7 = 8"). The same thing was done in the other operations.

4. Several relatively large whole number answers were a surprise, as in $\frac{3}{4} + \frac{1}{2} = 86$ (5 + 3 = 8; 4 + 2 = 6) or $\frac{3}{4} + \frac{1}{2} = 59$ ("4 and 5 is 9; 3 and 2 is 5"), or $\frac{3}{8} + \frac{7}{8} = 26$ ("7 over 8 is 15; 3 over 8 is 11; 15 + 11 = 26").

5. The numerator and denominator of one fraction were added for the numerator of the sum, and the same with the second fraction for the denominator of the sum, as in $\frac{3}{8} + \frac{7}{8} = \frac{11}{15}$ ("8 and 3 is 11; 7 and 8 is 15"), or $\frac{3}{4} + \frac{1}{2} = \frac{7}{7}$ ("3 + 4 = 7; 2 + 5 = 7"), or $\frac{2}{3} + \frac{1}{2} = \frac{5}{3}$ ("2 + 3 = 5; 2+ 1 = 3").

Subtraction

6. As in addition, a very prevalent practice was to subtract numerators for the numerator of the difference and the same with denominators; as in $\frac{3}{4} - \frac{1}{2} = \frac{2}{2}$ (3 − 1 = 2; 4 − 2 = 2); or $8\frac{2}{5} - 4\frac{3}{10} = 4\frac{1}{5}$ (8 − 4 = 4; 3 − 2 = 1; 5 from 10 is 5), or $7\frac{1}{2} - 4\frac{1}{4} = 3\frac{0}{2}$ (7 − 4 = 3; 1 − 1 = 0; 2 from 4 = 2), or $\frac{5}{8} - \frac{1}{3} = \frac{4}{5}$ (1 from 5 is 4; 3 from 8 is 5).

7. In writing equivalent fractions, some pupils divided a denominator into the C.D. and added this quotient to the numerator of the original fraction for the numerator of the equivalent fraction, as in $\frac{3}{4} = \frac{4}{4}$ (4 goes into 4 one time; 3 + 1 = 4). Others subtracted for the new numerator, as in $\frac{5}{8} = \frac{2}{24}$ ("8 goes into 24, three times, 3 take away 5 is 2").

8. As in addition, some surprising whole numbers were derived for answers, as in $\frac{3}{4} - \frac{1}{2} = 22$ ("2 take away 4 is 2; 1 take away 3 is 2"), or $8\frac{2}{5} - 4\frac{3}{10} = 394$ ("2 over 5 would leave 3; 3 over 10 would leave 9; 4 from 8 would leave 4"), or $7\frac{1}{2} - 4\frac{1}{4} = 133$ ("1 over 2 leave 1; 1 over 4 would be 3; 7 from 4 would leave 3").

9. There were cases of the wrong use of borrowing, as in $8\frac{2}{5} - 4\frac{3}{10} = 3\frac{9}{5}$ (borrowed 1 from 8; made it a 7; changed 2 of $\frac{2}{5}$ into 12; then $7\frac{12}{5} - 4\frac{3}{10} = 3\frac{9}{5}$), or $8\frac{2}{5} - 4\frac{3}{10} = 3\frac{1}{10}$ (wrote $\frac{4}{10}$ for $\frac{2}{5}$ and $\frac{4}{10}$ for $\frac{3}{10}$; "you can't subtract 4 from 4, so you borrow 1 from 4 [remainder from 8 − 4] make it a 3." Made first $\frac{4}{10}$ into $\frac{5}{10}$, then $\frac{5}{10} - \frac{4}{10} = \frac{1}{10}$).

10. A frequent error in writing equivalent fractions was to choose a C.D.; use it for the denominator of the new fraction but retain the numerator of the old fraction; as in $\frac{5}{8} = \frac{5}{24}$ and $\frac{1}{3} = \frac{1}{24}$.

11. The borrowed number was used incorrectly as in $9\frac{2}{3} - 5\frac{7}{8}$ rewritten as $9\ \frac{16}{24} - 5\frac{21}{24}$. Then $8\frac{26}{24} - 5\frac{21}{24}$.

Multiplication

12. Many pupils first wrote equivalent fractions, unnecessarily, and then incorrectly multiplied numerators and placed the product over the C.D., as in $\frac{2}{3} \times \frac{3}{5} = \frac{10}{15} \times \frac{9}{15} = \frac{90}{15}$, or $\frac{2}{3} = \frac{7}{15}$ ("3 goes into 15 five times; 5 + 2 = 7") and $\frac{3}{5} = \frac{6}{15}$ ("5 goes into 15 three times; 3 + 3 = 6"). Then $\frac{7}{15} \times \frac{6}{15} = \frac{46}{15}$ because 6 × 7 = 46, or $2\frac{1}{2} \times 6 = \frac{5}{2} \times \frac{12}{2} = \frac{60}{2}$.

13. Here, as in addition and subtraction, surprisingly large whole numbers were derived as products, as in $\frac{2}{3} \times \frac{3}{5} = 100$ ("2 × 5 = 10, put down 0 and carry 1; 3 × 3 = 9, + 1 = 10. Answer 100"), or $2\frac{1}{2} \times 6 = 120$ (wrote vertically with 6 below $2\frac{1}{2}$. Then "0 times $\frac{1}{2}$ = 0; there is nothing under $\frac{1}{2}$ so multiply by 0; 6 × 2 = 12, answer 120"), or $\frac{2}{3} \times \frac{3}{5} = 615$ ("2 × 3 = 6; 3 × 5 = 15").

14. In all the operations there were examples of correctly derived answers with errors introduced with conversions to simpler form, as in $2\frac{1}{2} \times 6 = \frac{5}{2} \times \frac{6}{1} = \frac{30}{2} = 15\frac{1}{2}$ ("2 goes into 30 fifteen times, and the denominator is 2"), or $\frac{2}{3} \times \frac{3}{5} = \frac{2}{3}$ ("$\frac{2}{3} \times \frac{3}{5} = \frac{6}{15}$, to reduce divide by $\frac{3}{3}$; 6 goes into 3 two times; 15 goes into 3 three times, so that'll be $\frac{2}{3}$").

15. Some pupils wrote the reciprocal of the second factor before multiplying, as in $\frac{2}{3} \times \frac{3}{5} = \frac{2}{3} \times \frac{5}{3} = \frac{10}{9}$, or $2\frac{1}{2} \times 6 = \frac{5}{2} \times \frac{1}{6} = \frac{5}{12}$.

16. In a mixed number times a fraction the fractions would be multiplied and the whole number affixed, as in $5\frac{1}{2} \times \frac{3}{4} = 5\frac{3}{8}$ ("1 × 3 = 3; 2 × 4 = 8; bring over 5"), or in $5\frac{1}{2} \times \frac{3}{4} = 5\frac{3}{2}$ ("$5\frac{1}{2} = 5\frac{2}{4}$ and $5\frac{2}{4} \times \frac{3}{4} = 5\frac{6}{4} = 5\frac{3}{2}$").

17. In a mixed number times a whole number the whole numbers would be multiplied and the fraction affixed, as in $2\frac{1}{2} \times 6 = 12\frac{1}{2}$ ("6 × 2 = 12, bring over $\frac{1}{2}$").

Division

18. As in multiplication a widely used practice was to divide numerators and place the product over the C.D., as in $\frac{9}{10} \div \frac{3}{10} = \frac{3}{10}$, or even in $\frac{7}{8} \div \frac{2}{3} = \frac{3}{2}$ ("2 goes into 7 three times; 3 goes into 8 two times"), or $15\frac{3}{4} \div \frac{3}{4} = \frac{6\cdot3}{4} \div \frac{3}{4} = 2\frac{1}{4}$.

19. After writing equivalent fractions errors were made in dividing numerators, as in $\frac{7}{8} \div \frac{2}{3} = \frac{21}{24} \div \frac{16}{24} = 1\frac{5}{24}$, or $\frac{21}{24} \div \frac{16}{24} = 1$ R5.

20. In dividing a mixed number by a whole number the whole number was divided by the whole number and the fraction was affixed, as in $6\frac{9}{10} \div 3 = 2\frac{9}{10}$.

21. In dividing a mixed number by a fraction, the fractions were divided and the whole number affixed, as in $15\frac{3}{4} \div \frac{3}{4} = 15\frac{1}{4}$ ("3 ÷ 3 = 1, bring over 15, the answer is $15\frac{1}{4}$"), or $15\frac{3}{4} \div \frac{3}{4} = 16$ ("$\frac{3}{4} \div \frac{3}{4} = 1$, bring over 15 and 15 + 1 = 16").

22. Numerators of like fractions were multiplied instead of divided, as in $\frac{9}{10} \div \frac{3}{10} = \frac{27}{10}$ ("the denominator would be 10; 3 × 9 = 27, and 27 would be numerator"), or in $15\frac{3}{4} \div \frac{3}{4} = 15\frac{9}{4}$ ("bring over 15; 3 × 3 = 9; bring over 4").

23. Numerators and denominators were multiplied without writing a reciprocal of the divisor, as in $6\frac{9}{10} \div 3 = \frac{69}{10} \times \frac{3}{1} = \frac{207}{10}$.

Helping Children Understand
Our Numeration System

Probably the chief reason children have difficulty with algorithms for whole number operations is that they do not have an adequate understanding of multi-digit numerals at the time they are introduced to the algorithms. Frequently, remediation of difficulties with computation is best accomplished by focusing upon the meaning of multi-digit numerals rather than upon the processes of computation.

Understanding our Hindu-Arabic numerals is *not* just "knowing place value." The concept of place value is important, but it is but one of many ideas children need to know if they are to understand multi-digit numerals and learn computational procedures readily. One of Glennon and Wilson's content objectives illustrates this well: "The number named by a multi-digit numeral is the sum of the products of each digit's face value and place value."[1] The terms used in this definition alert us to a number of ideas which are chained together in a functional understanding of multi-digit numerals.

If a child is to understand multi-digit numerals, he must first have some understanding of the operations of addition and multiplication. He must also be able to distinguish between a digit and the complete numeral. An understanding of a digit's face value involves the cardinality of the numbers zero through nine. The idea of place value involves the assignment of a value to each position within a multi-digit numeral; that is, each place within the numeral is assigned a power of ten. We, therefore, identify and name the tens place and the thousands place. This rather specific association of place and value is independent of whatever digit may happen to occupy the position within a given numeral. Usually, children having difficulty can identify and name place values, but they cannot go the next step. They have not learned to combine the concepts of face value and place value. It is the *product* of a digit's face value and its place value (sometimes called "total value of the digit")

---

[1]Vincent J. Glennon and John W. Wilson, "Diagnostic-Prescriptive Teaching," *The Slow Learner in Mathematics,* 35th Yearbook of the National Council of Teachers of Mathematics (Washington, D. C.: NCTM, 1972), p. 299.

which must be used. The sum of such products is the value of the numeral, and, in renaming a number, these products of face value and place value must continually be considered.

When teaching children our numeration system, we should introduce numerals as a written record of observations made while looking at or manipulating objects. For multi-digit numerals, these observations frequently follow manipulating the materials according to accepted rules in order to obtain the fewest pieces of wood (or the like), and, thereby, representations for the standard or simplest name for a number are obtained.

In all activities where children associate a numeral with materials, it is important that they have opportunities to go both ways. Children may be given materials to sort, regroup, trade, etc., and then they record the numeral that shows how much is observed. At the same time, children need to be given multi-digit numerals to interpret by constructing a set of materials which shows how much the numeral means. The ability of a child to go from objects to symbol and also from symbol to objects is an important indicator that the child is coming to understand the meaning of multi-digit numerals.

There are many aids available for numeration instruction, most of which are also used for demonstrating computational procedures. If teachers consider these aids carefully, they will recognize that many require very little understanding of concepts such as face value and place value, while others require the application of more complex ideas. The concepts of many-for-one and one-for-many equivalencies are difficult for young children, and the use of specific instructional aids may or may not involve these ideas.

Reflection upon these matters suggests a possible ordering of instructional aids for use with children in numeration work. Consider the following categories determined by what is done when a collection increases beyond nine single items.

Category 1   Objects which are placed in sets of ten. This may involve stacking chips, bundling sticks, or the like.

Category 2   Objects which are traded for a larger object which looks like a set of single objects glued together. Such materials include sticks used in a way where there is no bundling but only trading for already made bundles; it also includes base ten blocks and the like.

Category 3   Objects which are traded for a single object the same size and shape as a unit object but are distinguished from the unit object by color or by both color and place. Many chip-trading activities fit this category, as does a computing abacus with a different color for each place.

Category 4   Objects traded for a single object identical to the unit object but distinguished from the unit object *only* by the placement of the object. Such instructional aids include many place-value charts and devices as well as a computing abacus which has discs of only one color.

Instruction in numeration often involves children with instructional aids in Category 4 too early, and they merely learn complex mechanical procedures for getting answers. The use of varied instructional aids in a sequence similar to that suggested above may do much in helping children relate numerals to appropriate collections in their environment.

APPENDIX D

Sample Learning Hierarchy for Addition of Unlike Fractions

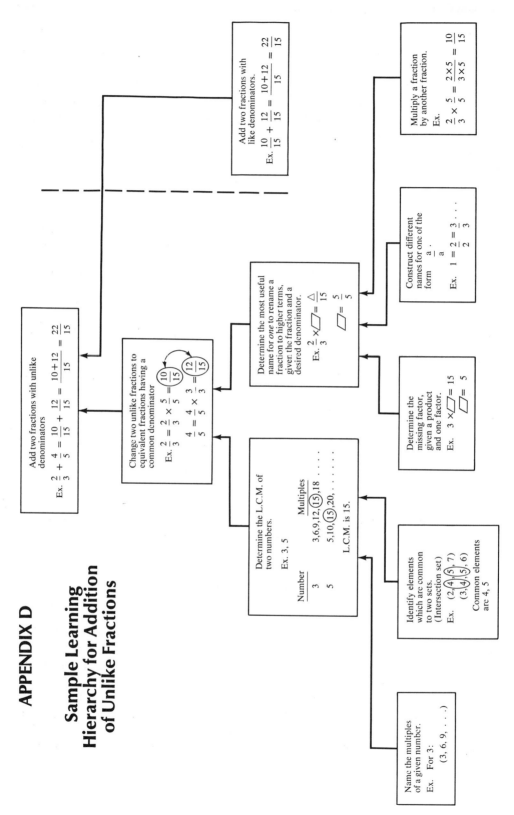

Selected Materials for Remedial Instruction

Description of Materials

Arithmablocks

This is a set of blocks and rods designed primarily for use in teaching addition and subtraction concepts. The materials are especially useful for helping children learn addend pairs for a given sum. Available from Great Ideas, Inc.

Base 10 Blocks

These blocks include a small cubic unit, long blocks which are 10 units long, flat square blocks which are the equivalent of ten of the 10-unit blocks, and large cubes which are the equivalent of 1000 units. Available from Creative Publications and Math Shop, Inc. (The following materials from the Cuisenaire Company of America, Inc., constitute a set of base 10 blocks: white rods, orange rods, orange squares, and orange cubes.)

Chip Trading Activities

This program is a sequence of games, problems, and other activities involving the trading of colored chips. The activities emphasize the concept of place value, patterns in numeration, decimal notation, regrouping in addition and subtraction, multiplication and division processes, and numeration systems other than base ten. Available from Scott Resources, Inc., and Creative Publications.

Cover Up

This is a game which provides practice with basic addition facts, specifically, recalling addend pairs for a given sum. It is especially enjoyed by children because of its manipulative feature and the need to use a bit of strategy. Available from Sigma Scientific, Inc.

Cuisenaire Rods, Squares, and Cubes

These materials are colored rods and blocks which can show units and higher powers in base ten and other bases. They have a great variety of potential uses. Available from Cuisenaire Company of America, Inc.

Fraction Bars

The generic term *fraction bar* is frequently applied to rectangular unit regions which are partitioned and used to represent fractions. However, there is an instructional program entitled Fraction Bars, a program involving games, manipulative materials, workbooks, tests, and other activities. The fraction bar model is central to the program. Available from Scott Resources, Inc., and Creative Publications.

Fraction Blocks

These blocks vary in size according to specific ratios and can represent fractional parts of any block defined as the unit. Many kindergarten building blocks meet this criterion, as do Cuisenaire Rods. Available from Creative Playthings, Inc.

Fractional Parts of Unit Regions

These are usually circular or rectangular regions separated into parts of equal area. They may be "pies" or "cakes," felt pieces, or made from poster board. Available generally from school supply companies.

Fractionrods

This is a set of blocks designed primarily for teaching fraction concepts and equivalent fractions. Available from Great Ideas, Inc.

Hainstock Blocks

Each plastic block contains a set of balls and is clearly marked with a numeral to show how many balls are in the set. The unique feature of the blocks is that the set of balls can be partitioned in many different ways, thereby illustrating addend pairs for a given sum. The fact that the blocks are highly manipulative and just a bit noisy makes them even more desired by children. Available from Creative Publications and Math Shop, Inc.

Heads Up

Heads Up is a game which provides practice with the basic facts of arithmetic. Immediate recall is encouraged in a relaxed setting. Available from Creative Publications and Sigma Scientific, Inc.

Math Balance

This is a highly motivating aid for teaching the fundamental operations of arithmetic. It can be used for exploring open-ended problems or for solving specific equations. The fact that it provides immediate confirmation makes it particularly effective for reinforcement activities. Available from suppliers generally.

Modern Computing Abacus

This device is an abacus with at least 18 discs on each rod. Children can show *both* addends before combining and trading. Some form of clothespin-like device is often used to separate sets of discs (the addends). Available from many school supply companies.

Multibase Arithmetic Blocks

Base 10 blocks are one example of a set of Multibase Arithmetic Blocks, but sets are also available for other number bases. Available from Creative Publications and Math Shop, Inc.

Place-Value Chart

This is a chart, or series of charts, in which positions are labeled as ones, tens, etc.; and cards or tickets placed within each position are assumed to have the value assigned to that position. Available from many school supply companies.

Prime Drag

This is a board game providing practice in deciding which of the numbers 2-100 are prime and which are composite. The game is exceptionally interesting for children because it is a race and includes highly varied activities. Available from Creative Publications.

Stern Blocks

These colored rods and other materials are designed to help children understand basic number relationships and the meaning of operations on whole numbers. Available from Houghton Mifflin Co.

Addresses of Distributors

Creative Playthings, Inc., Princeton, NJ 08540
Creative Publications, Box 10328, Palo Alto, CA 94302
Cuisenaire Company of America, Inc., 12 Church St., New Rochelle, NY 10805
Great Ideas, Inc., Box 274, Commack, NY 11725
Houghton Mifflin Co., 53 West 43rd St., New York, NY 10036
Math Shop, Inc., 5 Bridge St., Watertown, MA 02172
Mind/Matter Corp., Box 345, Danbury, CT 06810
Scott Resources, Inc., Box 2121, Fort Collins, CO 80521
Selective Educational Equipment (SEE), Inc., 3 Bridge Street, Newton, MA 02195
Sigma Scientific, Inc., Box 1302, Gainesville, FA 32601